THE VILLAGE SERIES

Cotswold Villages
June Lewis

Cumbrian Villages
Kenneth Smith

Devon Villages
S. H. Burton

Kent Villages
Alan Bignell

Lancashire Villages
Jessica Lofthouse

Shropshire & Herefordshire Villages
George H. Haines

Suffolk Villages
Allan Jobson

Surrey Villages
Derek Pitt and Michael Shaw

Yorkshire Villages
G. Bernard Wood

Shropshire &
Herefordshire
Villages

GEORGE H. HAINES

Photographs by the author

ROBERT HALE · LONDON

PRINTED IN GREAT BRITAIN BY
CLARKE, DOBLE & BRENDON LTD.
PLYMOUTH

Contents

Illustrations

The stables at Shipton, with the dovecot behind
Upton Magna gathers around its green

Between pages 96 and 97
A view in Hope Dale at the southern end of Wenlock Edge
The doorway at Kilpeck church
The brass to Dame Margaret Chute at Marden
At work in the new Mortimer Forest
"Is my seam straight?"—a ploughing match
Emptying hops in the oasthouse for drying
Efficient handling speeds selling at Craven Arms

Between pages 112 and 113
The gatehouse at Stokesay seen through the church lychgate
Topiary at Woonton
Topiary at Stoke Prior
'Border Fan' corn dolly at Eye Manor
Vats at Weston's cider works
Goodrich Castle seems to grow out of the rock

Between pages 136 and 137
Black-and-white at Weobley
The massive detached belfry at Bosbury
The pagoda-like detached belfry at Pembridge
Clun church has a typical border-style tower
Culmington spire is topped with aluminium fins
The Italian-style campanile above Hoarwithy
At Eardisley a barn has been converted into homes
Brook House and its dovecot at King's Pyon
Old church at Llanwarne
New Catholic church at Ewyas Harold
Luntley Court—the dovecot and cottages
The church at Staunton is well above the Arrow

MAPS

Introduction

WHERE local loyalties are concerned one has to be very careful, even among friends. I sat for a long time wondering whether this book should be entitled *Shropshire and Herefordshire Villages* or *Herefordshire and Shropshire Villages*; and when it came to planning the chapters without appearing to give precedence to any one area the problem became even more difficult. Then I remembered the advice of the King in *Alice in Wonderland*, "Begin at the beginning and go on till you come to the end: then stop."

This simple formula suggested a suitable compromise and the book therefore begins at Acton Pigot where we lived when we first came into these border counties; circles round Shropshire and then round Herefordshire; and finally ends in the Vale of Arrow where we live now. I think that this is such a logical arrangement that it will appease all my friends in the two counties, and I hope that at the same time it will be convenient for others who are interested in the area.

I once wrote an article which described the pleasure of walking in the lanes round our Shropshire home and it was turned down by the editor of a well-known countryside magazine because he did not believe that it was possible to find lanes or places which were so peaceful these days. Some readers may feel the same on reading the descriptions of a number of these villages; but although a certain amount of the historic background of the places is given, the descriptions of them are as they were in 1973, for in order to ensure that the details were accurate I visited every village during that year.

Especially in the western halves of the two counties there is a peace which is unbelievable to those who do not know it. On my journeys around England I frequently find that some village or old town has changed completely since my previous visit to it; a place that was a delight has suffered a development which has buried its character under an intrusion of 'Uniplan' buildings. It is a relief to return to these border villages assured that here things will be unchanged.

The tide of progress can no more be halted than could Canute stop the incoming sea on the Sussex beaches; indeed if the country-side is to survive and continue to give us pleasure it is essential that our villages are helped to take their place in the twentieth century and not be preserved as museum pieces. Living in the country, I know only too well the troubles that can arise from inadequate water supplies, skeleton transport arrangements and a lack of shopping facilities. The towns and villages of the country-side must be brought up to date, but the changes should be carried out with due feeling for their character. This was done in the past and is the reason why we have such a rich heritage of villages. Surely with the improved techniques of today we can do as well? There must be more regard for the long term effect and less for the speculator's quick and easy profit. Progress must bring improvements to the villages, not mark the ruin of something which has taken many centuries to create.

There is an integrity in this countryside of the borderland which we cannot afford to lose. A farmer can be sure that his men will do a good day's work in the fields although no one will see them from morning to dusk. When our village shop changed hands the new owner was astonished to be told by customers, "If I'm not in when you come go round to the back. The door will be open and you'll find the money on the kitchen table."

This other-worldliness is one of the great charms of the border counties, especially of south Shropshire and Herefordshire, and it suggests a detachment from the normal run of life.

The reason is basically geographical, for it is here that the low land of England meets the mountains of Wales in a natural boundary that has been recognized for many centuries. On the east

side we are not quite so secure. Cheshire and Staffordshire merge
into north Shropshire and there is an industrial fringe around
Wellington and the new town of Telford. Further south, the Severn
with the Clee Hills, the Malverns and the Woolhope Hills, form
a barrier which protects the area and restricts traffic to a few
arteries. In the hilly districts, the slopes are usually steep so that
most roads follow the valleys and few cross the ridges. This tends
to create tight communities; the folk who live over the hill
may be only a few miles away, but it is very difficult to meet
them.

Historically the area owes much of its isolation and special
characteristics to the creation of the Marcher Lordships by
William the Conqueror. To hold this troublesome border region
William granted lordships, the chief of which were the earldoms of
Herefordshire, Shropshire and Cheshire, based on Hereford, Shrewsbury and Chester, to some of the men who had helped him with
the invasion. He thus rewarded them with land which he himself
had only recently acquired, and also saddled them with the task
of keeping the Welsh in Wales. This created a series of buffer states
that gradually extended into a belt that spread out on either side of
the boundary and was fifty miles deep in places.

It is believed that at one time there were as many as 143 lordships in which the lords owed fealty to the king, but exercised
feudal power in military, judicial, economic and social spheres,
so that the areas were apart from the rest of the country in most
ways. Death, failing lines, marriage and the hazard of falling into
royal disfavour meant that there were changes in the individual
lordships from time to time, but they lasted for nearly 500 years
till the Act of Union in 1536 created the new Welsh counties of
Flintshire, Montgomeryshire, Radnorshire, Breconshire, Glamorgan
and Monmouthshire, and at the same time reshaped Shropshire
and Herefordshire. However, they did not finally die out for another 150 years when the office of Lord President of the Marches
and the Council of Wales and the Marches were abolished in 1689.
Such a long period of apartness from the rest of England has bred
traditions, connections and characteristics which still exist, long

after the castles of the Marcher Lords have fallen into ruins and many of the great families have died out.

This is one reason why the counties are composed of small communities. Ludlow, claiming to be the largest town in south-west Shropshire, has a population of only 7,500 and Leominster, the second largest town in the whole of the county of Hereford-shire, has a similar population.

The villages are equally small in scale. Many would only pass as hamlets in other counties, but despite this they are real units with tight loyalties. Now a number of the schools have been closed, pubs have become private houses and even some of the churches have been declared redundant and offered for sale. Yet the tradi-tions of the villages are as strong as ever.

The countryside, too, is modest. There are no outstanding beauty spots, but much of the area has that quiet charm and peaceful domesticity which is traditionally 'English' but very hard to find these days.

The pace of life is slow. At times even we who live here com-plain that it is too slow, but we are the first to agree that if things changed, much that we value would be lost.

VILLAGE *The Concise Oxford Dictionary* defines a village as being 'larger than a hamlet and smaller than a town'. Pursuing the matter further, a town is defined as 'a considerable collection of dwellings etc. (larger than a village)'; and a hamlet as a 'small village, especially one without a church'.

In classifying places as villages for this book I have worked within these definitions. No place without a church is included as a village and some of the smallest with churches have also been considered as hamlets; places with their own urban councils in 1973 have been classed as towns and also several 'by ancient right' as explained in the relevant chapters.

Staunton-on-Arrow   G.H.H.

I

All Friends around the Wrekin

WE came to the border counties from the heart of Oxfordshire. It was a dramatic change to leave the flat plain west of Bicester for the hill-ringed skyline of Acton Pigot. Even our five-year-old daughter was fascinated by the new scene and often when she was missing, we would find her looking out of one of the upstairs windows and she would explain that she had been to see 'The Hill'.

Although it is only 1,334 feet high, and by no means the highest hill in Shropshire, the Wrekin is particularly striking because it stands in the plain south of Shrewsbury and is instantly recognizable. It provided a day-long show, changing colour from dawn to dusk, even appearing to vary in size according to the lighting conditions, and after dark in those days there was the now-extinguished red beacon on its top. For the years that we lived at Acton Pigot the Wrekin symbolized home—although in fact it was six miles from our house—and when we were returning from trips we felt we were on home ground once we had sighted it.

The old Shropshire toast 'To all friends around the Wrekin' expresses the significance of the hills locally. Just as Cockneys consider themselves to be the only true Londoners, so those round the Wrekin feel that they are the real Salopians, and those living in other parts of the county are thought of as lesser cousins.

In going to Shropshire we felt we were venturing into a faraway wild country and we were certainly foreigners to the local people. Our reception was kind enough and help was generous, but it was a long time before we felt we had broken through that invisible

SHROPSHIRE

barrier and been accepted. I was secretary on a farm and spent many days in the fields helping at haymaking and harvest time so that I built up with the men that fellowship which exists between those who work hard as a team, but I was still an outsider. Among other things I had to learn the peculiarities of Shropshire dialect: to be 'starved' did not mean to be hungry, but to be very cold; a 'pikel' was a pitchfork; and a 'dunnuck' was a dung fork.

This reserve was an inborn caution, for in the border hills a stranger may always be an enemy. Foreigners have always been potentially dangerous and it was a natural reaction to give them misleading information. When old Tom Dovey told me to beware of the village over the hill because it was a wild place where the sparrows flew backwards I knew that was a 'tale', but it was more difficult to recognize the invention when the herdsmen gave me the wrong name for a cow that had just calved. In time, however, I felt that I had been admitted as a Salopian—it was shown by a subtle turn in Norman's jokes, and by a change in the glint in Doug's eyes as he pulled less than his weight when we were tossing a bag of potatoes. They became friendly pranks rather than a way of keeping a foreigner in his place.

Not long ago I saw a criticism of a book on Shropshire which protested that some of the place names were mis-spelt. I have no doubt that the critic was theoretically right, but in rural districts the spelling of place names is still often as variable as that used in medieval times. I decided that to avoid such criticisms of this book I would use the spelling on the Ordnance Survey One Inch Sheets; and here I am in difficulties already, for I see that the latest sheet has 'Acton Pigott'. However, all the time that I was living there, the farm had 'Acton Pigot' on the letterheading, so I will use this form on the grounds of local knowledge.

Strictly, Acton Pigot does not qualify for this book as it is only a hamlet with a few cottages and a farmhouse down a lane that is too narrow for comfort. It is an outlier of Acton Burnell, which stands round a cross-roads by its park below a hill. Recently some of the cottages in Burnell have been smartened up and this has made its appearance less informal, but it is still peacefully modest and it comes as a surprise to find that it appears in encyclopedias under an entry "Acton Burnell, Statute of". That historic enactment calling upon debtors to pay their debts under the threat of having their goods seized and held till payment was made was passed way back in 1283. Edward I, who was busy fighting the Welsh at the time, called a Parliament which met in a large barn, the remains of which are still pointed out to visitors.

Acton Burnell did not gain this place in history by reason of its own importance, but because of the standing of one of its sons, Robert Burnell, who became Bishop of Bath and Wells and later of Winchester, and who was the king's confidant and adviser. Despite the fact that he had eighty-two manors Robert Burnell retained a special feeling for his home village and in 1284 he built the castle which, like Stokesay, was more a fortified house than a castle. Little now remains of this and the Department of the Environment does not even make an entrance charge, but what does still stand is sufficient to indicate that it was a grand building for its time, reflecting the power of its builder.

The standing of Robert Burnell is also shown by the church, for its proportions are too imposing for a small Shropshire village. The monuments add to the impression of dignity, especially the tomb chest with a brass to Sir Nicholas Burnell, and the later memorials to the Lees of the sixteenth and seventeenth centuries who were then owners of the estate. This later passed to the Smythes, a Catholic family, who built the fine hall standing near the church and castle. This was rebuilt after a fire in 1914 and was in use as a Convent School when we were there, but is now a Concord College.

Apart from this group of buildings at the east end, Burnell is a typical quiet village where changes occur slowly. When I passed through recently I noticed that the old forge where Ernie Higgs used to work was closed. He was one of the last to cling to the old ways, and round the walls of the smithy he kept the tools made by his father for such jobs as fashioning the fancy points of railings. When beet-hoeing time came round the men on our farm were always keen to have one of the special hoes Ernie fashioned from old files for they kept their edge much longer than lesser tools.

The peace enjoyed by Acton Burnell is largely due to the fact that it is so buried in the countryside. Even the cross-roads is a false promise: the east arm leads only to the house and the church, and the road to the south soon narrows as it goes through the hills to Langley, where there is a little seventeenth-century chapel with some simple benches and plain box pews. It is no longer used for services and is in the care of the Department of the Environment, looking rather forlorn.

In the triangle south of Shrewsbury, between the A49 and the A458, are several places which were among the first in the county that we explored and therefore always think of as rather special. Beyond Acton Pigot, over the hill past Golding and down the steep and very narrow Golding Lane, is Cound, a happy place of black-and-white cottages, a fine church and a school. This was a typical two-class village school, which did not even have electric light, but it had an enthusiastic teacher who encouraged our daughter to clear that terrifying eleven-plus hurdle and so eventually to get a university place at a time when entries had not reached their present huge scale. The school has now been closed because it was considered too small and the local children get mass education at a larger establishment. In many villages the same thing is happening and the loss to the local community spirit is very great. Perhaps some of the little schools were not too successful, but many of them were very good and their teachers were also very useful members of the community.

Cound church has some engraved copper plates, a variation of the more usual brasses, and some fine monuments to the Cressetts who lived at Cound Hall, a large brick house built in 1704. Out on the main road by the Severn is the 'Cound Lodge' Inn. Originally built for travellers on the river, it became a girl's school at one time, a change which must have puzzled the old beams. Perhaps the spirits were too strong, for it has now reverted to an inn and is a favourite with fishermen.

From Burnell, a road goes down the middle of the triangle, and this is the way that the older folk of the village could still remember going to Shrewsbury in the so-called bus, which was the local carrier's horse-drawn cart with boards fitted as seats. By the time we were there, travel had become up-to-date for there was a bus service run by the Davies Brothers. A couple of miles along the road is Pitchford with a little group of cottages of every type and the church at the end of a long drive by Pitchford Hall, which is surely Shropshire's finest black-and-white house. It was built in the mid-sixteenth century for Adam Ottley and has none of the curved decoration found on many buildings near the Cheshire border, but achieves a dazzling effect by the use of diagonally placed struts across the frame. Seen across the green of the park it makes an imposing sight—so much so that we were almost deterred from continuing on our first trip there when we went to buy some fruit from the garden! The little church by the house has one of the rare wooden figures, perhaps an early Pitchford, but the incised alabaster slabs of sixteenth-century members of the family are really more interesting because they show very clearly details of the dress of the period.

To the west is Condover, home of one of the most typical Shropshire characters, Richard Tarlton, who left his job of looking after pigs to be jester in Queen Elizabeth's court. He is said to be the character referred to by Hamlet in the lines in the graveyard scene, "Alas, poor Yorick!—I knew him, Horatio; a fellow of infinite jest, of most excellent fancy." I can well imagine him amusing the court with shrewd Salopian wit and craftily gauging the limit to which he could safely go. There are men like him to be found on the farms of Shropshire today. Mostly they are too modest to display their talents in public, but if they could be persuaded to do so Shropshire might be as famous as Merseyside for its comedians.

Today Condover is a very respectable village and there is no sign of Tarlton, who is buried at Shoreditch where he had been an innkeeper in later years. The big house, now a school for the blind, was built in the late sixteenth century for Thomas Owen,

Justice of Common Pleas, but it has been much altered. The village is a pleasantly modest place with pretty corners which tempt the camera, but never quite come up to expectations when the prints are made—a sure sign that much of the attraction is in the atmosphere, for the camera is an unemotional instrument which starkly records the bare facts in front of it.

There is a nice group of cottages leading up to the red sandstone church which fits neatly into the scene, without dwarfing the rest of the buildings; but this is because it is set well back for them, for when it is approached its size becomes apparent. Inside it seems even bigger and the great roof is impressively supported on hammerbeams. The wealth and power of the families of the district in the past is shown by the number of imposing memorials, including a lofty monument showing Dame Jane Norton, who died in 1640, facing her husband at a prayer desk, with her father and brother below. A rather theatrical monument showing Sir Thomas Cholmondeley kneeling is said to be the first sculpture by G. F. Watts; and near to it is the figure of Alice Cholmondeley (who died in 1868) which was carved by her husband Reginald who was one of Watts' fellow pupils. The inscription, "Reginald always standing by, carved me with his own hand", conveys something of the personal struggle of the young husband as he worked on this delicate figure.

A few miles to the east is Berrington, a delightful place which seems hardly to have changed in the twenty years since I first discovered it. It is a richly warm village with red brick cottages, mainly brick infilling to the timber-framed houses and a rich red sandstone church with a great tower that soars up like a cliff. Berrington still has cobbled pavements in places and at dusk when there is no traffic and the TV aerials cannot be seen it is almost like a stage set. Unfortunately, except on rare days, the church is very dark inside so that it is difficult to appreciate the carving. There is also an air of mystery about the true name of the battered wooden effigy in the church which is known locally as 'Old Scriven'.

It is a surprise to find the main Shrewsbury road only a mile away at Cross Houses, for Berrington seems deep in the heart of the country. A road goes down by the Severn to Atcham, where a new bridge has been built for modern traffic and John Gwynne's eighteenth-century bridge has been kept beside it, a pleasant example of conservation from the 1920s. Atcham hardly qualifies as a village, although until the recent reorganization it was the name of a large rural district with a record of well thought out schemes. The village is shattered by the constant traffic along the busy A5 road and its main features are the 'Mytton and Mermaid' Hotel in a fine red brick Georgian house, and Attingham Hall, now owned by the National Trust, most of which is used as an adult education college. The church stands away from all the activity, making a rather fine picture by the river. It is dedicated to St. Eata, from whose name both Attingham and Atcham are derived. The church has a curious collection of features from other places: there is a stained glass window from Bacton in Herefordshire showing Blanche Parry who served at Queen Elizabeth's court; there are Flemish panels in the pulpit and German ones in the reading desk; an incised monument to Edward Burton of Longnor Hall came from St. Chad's in Shrewsbury; and some of the stones at the base of the tower are Roman, probably from Viroconium at Wroxeter, two miles away.

Viroconium has been plundered for stone for building over the centuries since the Romans left and the team at present excavating the site are using the lines of trenches dug by the stone robbers to plot the shapes of the buildings that were there. When Thomas Telford first came to Shrewsbury he was so perturbed at the removal of stone at the time that he investigated the site for his employer Sir William Pulteney, who then owned it. Excavations have been going on for many years, but so far the most exciting feature is still the Old Work which has been visible for centuries.

The modern village of Wroxeter down by the Severn is an undistinguished place, where more stones from Viroconium have been used. The pillars of the church gateway are Roman columns; the font appears to have been adapted from another column; and some of the stones in the north wall are also from the same source.

Eyton on Severn was the birthplace of a truly colourful character, Edward Herbert, Lord Herbert of Cherbury (a variation of Chirbury), who lived from 1583 to 1648 and not only served as Ambassador in Paris, fought under the Prince of Orange in the Netherlands and suggested the marriage of Prince Charles and Henrietta Maria, but also wrote philosophical works which were highly regarded in his day and are still seen as important landmarks in the history of thought.

From Pigot our usual approach to this area was by going down to the A458 road at Cressage and crossing the bridge over the Severn there. The road from Shrewsbury here runs in a long stretch known locally as the Cressage Straight which was a favourite place for trying out the speed of cars and motorcycles. Along this stretch was the Lady Oak under which Dean Swift is said to have married a man and a woman with whom he was sheltering in a thunderstorm; the old tree eventually became decayed and hollow, but a young oak is now growing to replace it. The village takes its name from another tree, Christ's Oak, which has now completely vanished; this was one of the many trees under which St. Augustine is said to have preached. Despite these early associations, the village has the appearance of a recent development and even the church with its strange tower and pinnacles was only built in 1841.

Over the modern concrete bridge, the Wrekin grows in size till there is a fine view of it at the approach to Eaton Constantine where the road climbs up through a pleasant mixture of cottages and small houses. The church here was rebuilt just over a hundred years ago and fits in with the scene better than the one at Cressage because it is not so ambitious and has a modest bellcote rather than a tower. Surprisingly, for such a late restoration, it has retained its box pews. The showpiece—although not a showplace—of Eaton Constantine is the timber-framed Baxter's House where Richard Baxter the Puritan theologian was brought up as a boy. Baxter was one of the unfortunate moderates caught up in the extreme emotions of the Civil War; and while he accepted a chaplaincy in the Parliamentary Army he opposed the execution of the King and the vesting of supreme power in Cromwell. Later his refusal to accept the extreme religious views of the period brought him before Judge Jeffreys and he spent a period in prison which ruined his health.

Between the southern end of the Wrekin and the Severn is the village of Leighton. It is a delightful tree-shaded place with some black-and-white cottages that really deserve the term 'pretty' and a good-looking pub, the 'Kynnersley Arms'. Both the present Hall and the church which is in its grounds date from the eighteenth century and because they are of brick look even younger. But the Leightons were an old family and in the church there is an effigy of a knight, believed to be more than 600 years old, which was brought from Buildwas Abbey, and an incised slab to William Leighton, who died in 1520, and his wife. In such a rural setting it is a surprise to see cast-iron tomb slabs in the floor and, by the gate, the cast-iron tomb of Cornelius Reynolds who died in 1828. These are reminders of the days when Leighton was engaged in the iron industry, the ore and coal being brought from Lawley and Dawley. Now there is no sign of industry and the village sleeps peacefully under its trees. Mary Webb, the best-known Shropshire novelist, was born here, but she and her work really belong to the hills and the next chapter.

Shropshire does not have many thatched roofs, so those which are to be seen are particularly appreciated. Many are the work of Percy Hopcraft of Garmston who retired not so long ago. He was attracted to the craft in 1922 when he saw his father's house in Warwickshire being thatched and he took it up as a full-time job when he left the army in 1927. Percy was an individualist in the way of tools and the leggatt he used to knock the thatch into place was studded with horseshoe nails instead of being ridged in the traditional fashion. This meant that it could be used in any direction. Equally unusual was his knife which was a shortened bayonet—a nice version of the 'swords into ploughshares' theme and very appropriate in view of his years in the army.

The traveller going hopefully along the road by the river towards Buildwas gets a horrid shock as he turns a corner just above
Leighton for—although certainly there is the expected view of the
valley—stealing the scene are the two Ironbridge power stations,
the newer one having three huge cooling towers and a chimney
650 feet high. This is sited just outside the boundary of the Shropshire Area of Outstanding Natural Beauty and can be seen imping-
ing on the scene in many places miles away. No doubt there are
official reasons for its existence at this spot, but it cannot inspire
the people of the area to do their part in caring for the countryside.

The village of Buildwas in growing quickly and not too un-
kindly behind its tiny church to which an appealing little timber-
framed belfry was added in the nineteenth century. Buildwas is
best known for the remains of the Abbey over the river. This was
founded about 1150 and there is still sufficient left of the nave
for it to be appreciated. Unlike many abbeys, Buildwas is quite
modest in size, and when it was built the site must have been
idyllic. The river is now crossed here by a very ordinary bridge
which replaced one built by Telford in 1795–6 which was as
noteworthy as the more famous one at Ironbridge, for it was
a step forward to a real appreciation of the use of iron for
bridges.

Although its span was 130 feet against the 100 feet of Darby's
bridge, it used only 173 tons of iron instead of the 378 tons used
by its predecessor. Perhaps this did not please the ironmasters
who were looking for extra sales of iron, but it marked an important stage in bridge-building, where the weight of the bridge itself
is one of the great problems.

Telford New Town has swallowed up a number of villages in this
district, but it is reassuring to find that so far Little Wenlock
manages to preserve its peace despite the fact that it is perched
unpromisingly high above the 700-feet contour with signs of in-
dustrialism all around it. The old church was so extended in 1865
that now it seems to be merely an appendage to the Victorian
building, but it sits attractively in the centre of the churchyard

and the older houses gather round it to give Little Wenlock a quiet attraction.

A fine avenue of trees leads from the busy A5 road to Uppington which has also escaped so far. Its many brick houses create a rich contented air without any special posing. The church is right at the end of the village, as if the people could not decide where to put it. Here again restoration (in 1885) was so heavy that it is virtually a Victorian church but there is a tympanum over a blocked doorway with a dragon that looks Saxon, and the porch bears the initials of Francis Boycott with the date 1678. There is also a delightfully delicate window with a pattern of flowers in memory of twenty-five-year-old Lucy Priscilla Ashdown, which is a welcome change from the usual heavy religious subjects.

The feature which evokes most memories for me, however, is a large brass tablet placed on the wall in 1930 in memory of Goronwy Owen who was curate of the parish from 1740 to 1753. Goronwy Owen was born in Anglesey and owed his education to Lewis Morris who also helped him after he was ordained. His fame rests on his verse which was helped by being mentioned and praised by George Borrow. My father was a fervent reader of Borrow's *Wild Wales* and when I set out in 1929 on my first cycle tour he asked me to take a picture of the poet's birthplace for him. In those days English was little spoken on Anglesey and I asked several people for guidance to no avail, till eventually the beautiful daughter of the local squire appeared at my tent door like an English-speaking vision and not only answered my queries but also took me to the birthplace. I've remembered her for forty-four years, and I must confess that I have never looked at one of Goronwy's poems. I really owe him that.

If the Wrekin was our first Salopian landmark, Wenlock Edge was our second, or more especially the steep climb up Harley Bank to Much Wenlock, for it was some years before we got to know the full length of this ridge which runs south-west nearly to Craven Arms. The steep climb has an early cycling memory too, because on a tour in the early 1930s, when I made my first acquaintance with the county, I got a puncture in the rear tyre

The road winds through Harley

Maiden's garland at Astley Abbots

Bench end carved by the vicar
at Middleton

Berrington is one of the least spoilt villages

From the south the Wrekin appears conical

From the west the Wrekin has a whaleback shape

Black-and-white at Bletchley—the left wing is painted brickwork

At Nesscliff the old school is now a studio

Home in a castle—Whittington Castle

A round home in the old toll house, Ruyton XI Towns

Busy green at Norton in Hales—the Bradling Stone is behind the seat

of my bicycle while pushing up Harley Bank, the surface of which was not then made up.

In those days, and until quite recently, the main-road traffic used to go through the little village of Harley, skirting the church wall and passing the turning with its often pictured signpost to Wigwig and Homer, and then dropping down before making the steep ascent of the Edge. When I recently revisited Harley I was puzzled by the lack of traffic in the village although I could see plenty on the hill in the distance. As I moved around the road to get the best angle for a photograph, I kept a very wary eye for cars but none came and I began to fear they were being swallowed up in a chasm at the foot of the hill, till a passing farm worker told me that a by-pass had been built. The effect of this is dramatic and shows how greatly traffic spoils villages, for now it is a place transformed and for the inhabitants life must be much more pleasant. To re-route all our roads is an impossibility and would spell ruin for many filling stations and roadside cafés, but the examples here and at Tong and Dilwyn show that it would be a dramatic way of improving the environment. Harley is built on an 'S' bend of the road with two minor roads coming in, but it makes up into quite an attractive place because it is built on a hillside and the slope gives interesting levels. The church stands above the cottages and although (apart from the tower) it was rebuilt in the nineteenth century it looks well. Here, as so often happened in my travels, I could not see the brasses in the church because of the activities of rubbers; this pastime is becoming such a cult that I feel that special hours should be set aside for it, or soon the ordinary visitor will be unable to see the brasses at all.

An alternative route from Cressage to Much Wenlock is by way of Sheinton which meanders along the road with no apparent formation. The church with its timber-framed belfry stands on a cliff-like bank from which there are intriguing birds-eye views of the farms and cottages. The church itself is now mainly Victorian, but it has a huge door which is out of scale with the rest of the building and is said to have come from Buildwas Abbey.

The road along the top of Wenlock Edge is a favourite view-

point for motorists, but as so often happens the views *to* the hill
are as striking as those from it and these can be seen by going
through the villages lying north of the Edge. At Kenley, the cottages and farms spread for quite a way along the road as if each
was intent upon getting a position with a good view. The little
church, which has a short tower and is whitewashed inside, stands
at the end of the village and from the churchyard there is a grand
stretch of countryside across to the Stretton Hills. Archibald
Alison, who was rector here, wrote *Essays on the Nature and
Principles of Taste*. He used to be visited by Thomas Telford and
it could have been his talks with the Scot which influenced him
to move to Edinburgh in the hope that his two sons would have a
better chance there. This was certainly a successful move because
one son, Sir Archibald, became a judge; and the other, William,
helped to improve the poor relief system. His little church now
has a new door—a rather rare sight.

Hughley church is famous for A. E. Housman's reference to
its steeple, when in fact it has a short tower with a timber belfry with
brick infilling, which houses a clock presented in 1892 by the Earl
of Bradford when his horse won the Derby. When he was taxed
about the steeple, Housman confessed that he had another place
in mind, but as it had an ugly name he had substituted Hughley
and had not expected that anyone would go to look for it. Now
there is a large crack in the tower and a notice warns that it is
dangerous to stand near it. Perhaps this is retribution for the
mis-statement.

It is a nicely rural village with cottages and farms which look
as if they were sited where they would look best without regard
to confining them to a built-up area or a rigid building line.
Farmyards spill out on to the road and everything is comfortable
and natural.

This is a fine stretch of countryside which rises up to Yell Bank
with many steep and narrow lanes, which are adventurous for
motorists and do not encourage exploration. There is however,
one excellent road running south-west from Hughley to a cross-
roads near Longville and on to Cardington, which gives splendid

views of Wenlock Edge and which will not worry even nervous drivers.

This passes Church Preen School. The village is over a mile uphill, which should be helpful for children who are late in setting out for the school in the morning. Surprisingly, in view of its elevation, Church Preen is set among trees.

Near the church is a group of new cedar-boarded houses which in themselves are quite attractive, but which suffer from the fact that it is difficult to plan informality, and they look terribly posed. With an estimated life of fifty years according to an architect I met, they will barely have enough time to settle down in this timeless countryside. The church was a cell of Wenlock Abbey for a period and this may have influenced its design, for it is very long and tall in relation to its width and, for worshippers, this creates something of the atmosphere of an abbey. There is a little cell-like south chapel which matches in so well with the rest of the building that it could be taken for the same age, but in fact it was built of old stones and added as memorial to the late owner of the manor house in the early 1920s.

Cardington is by far the largest of these villages under the Edge, but it is built on the same jumbled plan, although it does have two 'set pieces', the little square in front of the church and the fine grouping of the church and the 'Royal Oak' Inn below it. It is one of those places which can be explored for quite a time and which continually reveal new corners, and it is more like a mountain village than one in a valley.

The church has a tall tower and inside it is rather grand for such a cosy village, with a high roof with many beams. The clue, as so often happens, comes in the memorials, which show that there were grand folk there in the past. The grandest was obviously William Leighton who was Chief Justice of North Wales and one of the Council in the Marches of Wales. He lays in a crimson gown with his head resting on his hand, but the sculptor appears to have been defeated by his legs, for two little feet stick out horizontally from the bottom of his robe making it look as if the figure had toppled over. William Leighton built Plaish Hall in the late sixteenth century, when it was one of the earliest brick houses in the county and there is a story that a condemned man was employed to build the chimneys. There are also in the church many memorials to the Corfields who lived up at Chatwall Hall, which lies above the 900 feet line, a surprising height for an important house. I am intrigued by the neatly apportioned bequest of Roger Manncell recorded in the church: he left £1 6s. 8d. yearly for ever "to be disposed of three years to be laid out in bread for the poor; three years in wine for the communion; and ye seventh year for an ornament to ye church". Charity, Faith and Hope?

Rushbury, nearer to the Edge, has an arrangement which is quite common in the county, with the church in the centre of a square and the houses of the village built round the four sides. This is an old settlement, for there is a castle mound nearby, and a little packhorse bridge leads to Roman Bank, where there is be-lieved to have been a camp. Despite its age the church is rather plain inside.

I discovered Eaton under Heywood in one of my early journeys round Shropshire. It lies among trees very close to the foot of the Edge and there is just a scatter of cottages and a church which seems to have grown on its site; even the floor follows the natural rise of the ground to set the altar at the highest point. Inside it is rather gloomy because of the wealth of dark woodwork, some of which is said to have come from one of the old manor houses. In view of the fact that so many of the parishes are losing their incumbents now, it may encourage them to know that Eaton lost its status as a Rectory for many centuries, but this dignity was restored in 1868.

The richness of the area to the north of the Edge is seen at its best at Acton Scott, which lies by Acton Park with high hills all around, near enough to be impressive but far enough away not to cast gloom over the village. The Romans appreciated the merits of the situation and remains of their settlement have been found. The church is mainly medieval but was so restored in the eighteenth century that it has no air of any great age. Perhaps more impor-tant from a practical angle is the fact that its people still care for it, because the organ is new and the clock was presented to it in 1947. It is a typical manor church with memorials to the big families: a brass showing Thomas Mytton who died in 1577 with his family; then the Actons; and then the Stackhouse family which later became the Stackhouse-Actons.

Finally out on the road from Church Stretton to Much Wenlock, which is only a B road but seems very imposing after the by-roads explored in this chapter, is Hope Bowdler. It is built, as the 'Hope' of its name suggests, in a valley and climbs up a hillside with a delightful jumble of cottages and farms, almost in the way some Cornish villages huddle round their harbour. Traffic hurries through, but little change comes to the village. When I asked the vicar and his two companions what additions had been made in tht last ten years they could only think of one bungalow, the rectory and a few new buildings at the top of the village. The church, which is reached by an avenue of Irish yews, was rebuilt in the nineteenth century and has an almost too well-cared-for air.

Hope Bowdler is only just over the hill from Church Stretton and the Shropshire hills which are explored next.

The Villages of the Hills

ONE thing for which I shall always be grateful to this book is that it gave me the opportunity to see Shropshire as a whole in a relatively short period. Having lived within easy reach of Church Stretton and the Long Mynd for many years I had come to regard this area as being the 'essential Shropshire', a view which is also held by many visitors who only know the county from holiday trips. The many journeys which I have made recently have brought home to me the fact that the hills are actually only one side of Shropshire's attraction, and that they cover but a small proportion of its area. However, there is a special magic in the bare hills of south-west Shropshire and the little villages tucked among them, and the fact that the county has many other pleasant places does not detract from the delights of this area.

At the start of this chapter which deals with the hill country it is perhaps wise to include a reminder that our present concern is with the villages; some mention must be made of the surrounding countryside because it helps to create their atmosphere, but reference cannot be made to the more isolated areas of the hill country because they are beyond the scope of this book.

When we lived at Acton Pigot we took the road to the hills on many occasions. It was our target on that wonderful day that always comes early in the year as a promise of spring; in the heat of summer we went there looking forward to the breeze which is always to be found on the top of the Mynd; and in winter we went for the excitement of trying to climb the steep slopes when they were covered with snow.

After leaving Acton Burnell, the road picks up the line of a Roman way that comes from Viroconium and continues on past Church Stretton. To the south is Frodesley with its little church rebuilt in the nineteenth century. Then comes Longnor, remembered for its hump-backed bridge. For generations the Corbetts were the great local family; Sir Richard Corbett built the Hall in 1670, and in 1934 the Shropshire and West Midlands Agricultural Society presented new gates to the church in gratitude for the work that Lieut.-Colonel Corbett had done for the Society. The church is a tiny place tucked away among great trees, but it has a fine array of box pews, one dated 1723, and a two-decker pulpit. An unusual arrangement is the outside stone staircase leading to the gallery. Although this saves space it is a feature more often seen in farm buildings than in churches.

I have always had great difficulty in learning foreign languages and as an excuse I have advanced a theory that this is a gift that one either has or has not. A good example of the 'natural' linguist was Samuel Lee, born in Longnor in 1783. After starting work as a carpenter, in his spare time he learnt Latin, Greek and several other languages. Eventually he took up teaching and became Professor of Arabic at Queens' College, Cambridge, by the time he was thirty-six; later he was appointed Regius Professor of Hebrew. He translated the New Testament into Syriac and also did a translation of the Book of Job from the original Hebrew. He is the perfect illustration of my theory!

At 'Longnor turn' the lane comes out on to the busy A49 road which over the years has been slowly transformed along this section. For those who like this sort of road, it is an example of the great change that can be made by quietly working away at danger spots and improving them instead of waiting for the big scheme which never gets the necessary approval.

In the flat rather uninteresting country to the north there are a few villages on the way to Shrewsbury to look at before going into the hill country. First comes Dorrington, which is more important than it may appear to the motorist passing through, for quite a lot of it lies away from the main road. In an area which has so many old churches it is unusual to find one as new and urban looking as Dorrington's which was built in 1845. Like Longnor, Dorrington has its local boy who made good in a different line to that in which he started. John Boydell, born here in 1719, had been educated for the Church, but after a few years he left that profession and apprenticed himself to a London engraver. Within a short period he set up in business publishing his own engravings with some success, but his real fame came later when he published the work of other engravers, culminating in a series of Shakespearean subjects. The esteem in which he was held is indicated by the fact that he eventually became Lord Mayor of London. Much of his trade was with the Continent and his story almost ended sadly when financial difficulties caused by the European wars nearly ruined him, but he averted this disaster by disposing of his stock by lottery.

A couple of miles nearer to Shrewsbury, Stapleton lies back from the main road, a string of cottages and farms along a byway with a church which is probably unique, for it originally had two storeys. It was built in the late twelfth and early thirteenth centuries with an undercroft. In 1786 the two storeys were made into one and the result is a church with strange proportions. Two lines of windows, and details such as the old piscina now high in the wall indicate the two levels. The tower was added after the alteration, but in this also the proportions look wrong. A pretty feature of the church is a pair of candlesticks, believed to have come from Germany in about 1500, which stand six feet tall and are enamelled blue with gilt decoration.

Bayston Hill, like Dorrington has a church dating from the nineteenth century. This stands on one side of a large area of grass known as Bayston Hill Common, which is too large to be classed as a village green, for the houses standing on the other side look as if they are on a distant shore. The rest of the village is becoming a suburb of Shrewsbury, which is taking it out of our realm. Bayston Hill was probably a rather grand place in the late nineteenth century when the richer folk from Shrewsbury would set off in their carriages for the town, whose towers stand out across the intervening plain.

Southwards from the Longnor turn on the A49 lie the Church Stretton Hills with the line of the Long Mynd on the west of the road. This area has seen a change in the last fifty years. For centuries it was wild country with small farms eking out an existence; now it has been tamed by made-up roads and it is a target for weekend motorists. Farmers offer accommodation for visitors, and pony trekkers canter along the tracks which were only used by local folk in the past. But during many months of the year it reverts to its old character, like a farmer who puts on his working clothes after having dressed up in his best suit for a wedding.

The northern end of the Mynd is broader than the south and the gradients are less steep, but they are still sudden enough to cause concern to drivers from other parts of the country. The gateway to the hills is Leebotwood on the main road. The beautifully thatched 'Pound Inn' is a familiar landmark along the way which must have made more people aware of the existence of the village than anything else. In fact many of the cottages lie to the west of the road where the railway line still runs despite constant threat of closure. The church, which is a tidy little building with a small tower amid trees, stands at the end of the village on its own hillock, a sure sign of an early date. It does not promise much, but inside it has a range of box pews and a number of memorial tablets to the Corbetts of Longnor Hall. The walls are plastered, and recently a portion of the plastering became detached to reveal the earlier work with a tantalizing fragment of a wall painting believed to have been done when the church was built in 1181. An appeal fund has been started to restore this. Is it better to know that on the wall beneath the upper layer is an ancient painting or to risk damage by attempting to reveal all of it? Perhaps it is better partially exposed as a symbol of the age of the church; often the search for the facts destroys the essential magic.

c

From Leebotwood two roads go upwards to the hills. Smethcott and Picklescott are on a northerly route with far-stretching views, but a more interesting way is by Woolstaston where there is a little green and a gathering of cottages. This casual arrangement is typical of many villages in the county and strikes a contrast with the more precise type of layout seen in other parts of the country. Many Shropshire villages appear to have happened over the years rather than to have been the result of any definite plan, and the houses gain their unity as a result of growing old together like a happily married couple.

The church at Woolstaston is almost lost in the trees through which its bell turret can just be seen. In the dark interior is an unusual double font with an upright one standing in a broader lower type. Equally noticeable is the nineteenth-century carving of the woodwork. Thereby, as they say, hangs a story, for in fact the carving was paid for from the proceeds of the sale of a book-let, *A Night in the Snow*, which tells the story of how the rector, the Reverend Edmund Donald Carr, was lost in the snow on the hills above Woolstaston on 29/30th January 1865. This booklet was first published in 1865 but is still available now, as a reprint was published in 1970 by a local firm, the Onny Press.

Even in those days the practice of sharing rectors was in opera-tion and Mr. Carr served not only Woolstaston but also Ratling-hope on the other side of the Long Mynd. The two churches are four miles apart 'over the top', but twelve miles by roads round the base of the hills. Usually after holding a service at Wool-staston Mr. Carr had lunch, rode over to Ratlinghope to hold a service there and then returned to his home parish. No doubt this was often a pleasant trip and allowed him time to mull over his text, but when the weather was bad he had to walk, and it would be interesting to know the effect of such arduous journeys on his sermons.

On the 29th January 1865, the snow was deeper than it had been for many years and after morning service Donald Carr had a hasty drink of soup and set off for Ratlinghope. Conditions then were so bad that it took two hours to cover the four miles, and the people were surprised that he had made the trip. After the service the snow was even worse and the Ratlinghope folk pleaded with him to stay the night, but he set out on the return trip to take evening service at Woolstaston, impelled probably by that noble stubbornness that comes over us at such times, and also by the fact that he could not communicate with his house as this was in the pre-telephone era—though in such a storm today the lines would probably be out of action anyway.

The return trip started safely, but then in the blinding snow-storm he missed a landmark and made the common mistake of steering by the wind which gradually veered so that he headed southwards instead of east. The little book tells how for twenty-four hours he stumbled on, falling into ravines and losing hat, coat, boots and stick till after he had been blinded by the snow he was finally guided by the sound of voices to a house in Carding-mill Valley. Surprisingly this is all written in a most matter-of-fact style with none of the heroics that might be expected at that time. Indeed Donald Carr must have been an unusual man, because after only a quarter of an hour's rest he was off to Church Stretton and although a fly was able to take him to Leebotwood he had to walk the last part of the journey to Woolstaston. A search party of about thirty had been looking for him and had reported that he must have died in the hills. Oddly enough, on my last visit to Ratlinghope on a sunny day in autumn I was mulling over the fact that few modern visitors to the area could appreciate the diffi-culties of those days, when three army cadets came up to me and asked if I was going to Church Stretton because they were on an exercise and although it was broad daylight and they were equipped with an Ordnance Survey map, they had gone astray and were going to miss their lunch!

Ratlinghope, which is locally pronounced 'Ratchup', nestles in a valley on the west side of the Mynd and is so small, with only a few cottages and farms, that it hardly appears to merit Donald Carr's great efforts. The church has been much restored, but if the light is right it is just possible to read an inscription on the door, in a little panel with the words awkwardly broken to fit the space, to the effect that it was made and given by the churchwardens in 1625.

The main community along the west side of the Long Mynd is Church Stretton, a name many people use to cover All Stretton, Church Stretton, and Little Stretton which lie north to south in that order so closely that it is difficult to say where the dividing lines are, although each has its own character. They are fortunate in that the main-road traffic has gone along the route of the old Roman road on the other side of the railway for many years so that they have not been 'improved' in the interest of the motor car.

They were all typical little hill villages till Church Stretton began to develop as a health resort in the late Victorian period and it bears the hallmarks of that era with a number of well-built, ample houses. Church Stretton earned its prefix because until this century it was the only one of the trio to have a church, and this is a fine large building with two transepts. In one window is the figure of Jessica of *Jessica's First Prayer*, a Victorian best-seller by Sarah Smith, who was born in Wellington and took the pen-name of Hesba Stretton, which is made up from the initials of her brothers and sisters and the name of the village where she had spent many happy holidays. Sarah not only wrote many best-sellers of a similar type but was also very active in promoting the foundation and early growth of the Society for the Prevention of Cruelty to Children.

Church Stretton is now much larger than either of its neighbours and has a number of shops and a small, almost neglected, market place; All Stretton got its stone church in 1902 and has several good black-and-white houses; but Little Stretton is my favourite of the trio. It has a cosy position in a narrow valley and is a mixture of black-and-white and brick houses with the stone walls of small gardens fringing the road to give the village the true air of a place in the hills. It has a rather prim looking, thatched, black-and-white church which was built in 1903. The inside is lined with varnished wood so that it almost has the air of a sports pavilion, but it is saved by being consistent with a nicely conceived timber chancel arch and a wooden font.

The three villages are surviving very well, because their great attraction is the scenery, and most visitors pass through and either go to Cardingmill Valley or Ashes Hollow, two deepset valleys on the side of the Mynd, or else take the Burway road which climbs up the side of the great hill, at a gradient of 1 in 5 in parts, to the plateau-like top. Returning down this slope is a rather hair-raising experience for drivers with no head for heights because there is a precipice-like drop on the outside only a few feet from the road, and passing is very difficult. Many people prefer to go across the top and descend on the west side by the gliding station where, although the gradient is steeper, descending cars are on the inside. This also makes an excuse to watch the gliders. For many years most of them were launched by being pulled over the edg on elastic ropes by teams of stalwarts, which made an exciting sight, but now they are often launched by a winch. Once over the edge of the Mynd they are 1,300 feet up, but of course have to retain this 'bonus' height if they are to land on the club field.

West of the Mynd is a valley rising to an even more remote line of hills which begins with Linley Hill in the south and then rises to the higher Stiperstones. This end of the valley is a place of narrow lanes, fierce gradients and sharp corners. Among this maze of little ways, perched on a knoll, is Wentnor, with a Victorian church in which a lot of the old stones were re-used, and a group of cottages. Norbury, high up on the other side of the valley of the East Onny is a fortress-like place built to a pattern which becomes familiar in this district. The cottages, farms and a pub form a square round the outside of the churchyard. The church is another which was rebuilt in the nineteenth century, but the old tower, which looks as if it was originally built with defensive purposes in mind, was retained and given a new broach spire. I was wondering how a parish in such an isolated position could support itself when I saw a notice in the porch which showed that the profit from the 1973 fête had been £350. While the local folk care enough about their churches to arrange and support efforts on this scale there is no justification for closing them as redundant. In such places, the church is an essential feature of village life and as Ivor Bulmer Thomas of the Redundant Churches Fund said, 'by just being there it is a reminder of Christian principles."

On my recent trip here I became impatient with my maps and went adrift in the lanes, so I stopped to ask an old pensioner the way. He was very helpful, but I had to scale his instructions down to local dimensions: the 'signpost' he mentioned turned out to be a board pushed in the hedge; and the 'main road' he had raised my hopes with was a lane a little wider than the others on which two cars might pass if they held their breath. Seeking out these hill villages is an adventure.

A road follows the East Onny along this valley past Bridges with a Youth Hostel, a decorative inn and a turning which goes to Ratlinghope. Then there is a precipitous drop at Cathercott Hill to Castle Pulverbatch where the 'White Horse' Inn has a boastful doggerel on a board in its porch:

> Cathercot upon the hill
> Wilderly down in the dale
> Churton for pretty girls
> And Pulverbatch for good ale.

Castle Pulverbatch and Church Pulverbatch sit on neighbouring hills. Castle Pulverbatch has the motte of an old castle and Church Pulverbatch has the church. Both places are now being built up, for although they appear to be in wild country, they are only seven miles from the Shrewsbury by-pass. The results are not flattering to modern architects. But Church Pulverbatch still has a fine group of brick farm buildings at the top of the hill with the church lying back so that although its tower is prominent, it is approached by paths over rough grass. A picture of it in 1653 shows that it was then a simple building with a bellcote, but since then the tower was added in 1773 and it was largely rebuilt in 1853.

The way to Habberley is along a very narrow lane, but is worth the trip for the village is a charming oasis in the hills with a few farms and cottages and a trim pub called the 'Mytton Arms' after the Myttons who lived in the Hall; William Mytton was an eighteenth-century Shropshire historian of some renown.

The road comes out for breath at Pontesbury. I used to visit Pontesbury frequently some fifteen or more years ago and thought I knew what to expect. How wrong I was. The tower of the church was still there, but instead of looking over the old houses I remembered, it now stands among a quite large assemblage of modern houses and bungalows, another reminder of the nearness of Shrewsbury. It was strange to go into the church and see once more the fine sailing ship on the monument of Thomas Davies, and the marble figures on the reredos still unchanged even though the surroundings have altered so much. This has occurred in many villages over the centuries, but it is surprising to find it happen so quickly almost before your eyes. Perhaps, as in other places, everything will settle down again in time, for it seems a pleasant place to live.

Mary Webb who did so much to put Shropshire on the literary map with her novels lived at Rose Cottage which is now much altered and has been renamed Roseville. It was here in 1914 that she wrote *The Golden Arrow* one of her best-known books. Readers of this and of *Precious Bane* or *Gone to Earth* may regard them as period pieces, but time runs slowly in the hills of Shropshire. Walk around some of the lonely places of the Stiperstones and you will find the strange atmosphere that haunts the novels. And in remote places even today there are characters who might have stepped from her pages. Mary Webb was uniquely placed to catch the brooding atmosphere and put it on paper. To do this successfully demands a certain affinity with the surroundings combined with the detachment of an onlooker. Mary Webb was born in Shropshire, but her early days were spent in the softer eastern part of the county with the hills always on the distant skyline, so that she knew them well but was not of them. She came from a good middle-class family and married a Cambridge graduate who was a schoolmaster, yet while at Pontesbury she walked to Shrewsbury to sell the produce of her garden. In this way she was a finely tuned receiver of the atmosphere which her talent and years of endeavour at mastering words enabled her to put on paper.

In her novels the local places are thinly disguised: Shrewsbury becomes Silverton; the Long Mynd, Wilderhope; the Stiperstones, the Daifol Mountains; Condover, Conder.

Reaction to atmosphere is a personal thing so that it is difficult to recommend a place which appeals to oneself because it may not strike any note for others. But I will take a chance and suggest a visit to the Stiperstones country. There is a road which leaves the Minsterley/Bishop's Castle road to climb up past a Forestry Commission plantation to Shelve, where cottages and church stand up on the banks like sheep that have scrambled out of the way of the traffic. It is a delightfully higgledy-piggledy sort of place which at 1,150 feet claims to be among the highest parishes in England. It is one of those villages which show why planning can never create real atmosphere—Shelve could not be made, it could only happen. The situation is so unfriendly that it seems impossible that the village could exist for long, yet in the tiny church there is a list of vicars going back to 1349. In fact the earliest church is believed to have been erected in 1200 and the old font and some other features were re-used when the church was rebuilt in 1839.

Beyond Shelve there is a desolate waste over to Pennerley and the Stiperstones. The Devils Chair of the Golden Arrow legend stands out on the skyline. On a sunny day it looks a nice place for a picnic, but go there at dusk or as the storm clouds roll up and it is a place to awaken strange feelings. The ghosts of this waste are the miners who in the past have tried to win lead and other metals from the hills. There are Roman mines and evidence of efforts right through the ages. At Bog primitive shafts stand derelict. The miners came and then went, but the hills still stand.

Towards Shrewsbury there is Hope, in the valley as its name suggests, with houses scattered on the slopes on either side of the road and, in an enchanting situation, a nineteenth-century church which is approached over a little bridge.

And so down to Minsterley where a large dairy is growing up to dominate the village which now hardly lives up to its sweet sounding name, so that it brings one down to earth and dispels all the disturbing thoughts roused on the hills. Minsterley has an air of 'might have been' about it. All round hill ranges upon hill, but in the village one is safely on level ground and even the little brook is securely kept within ordered bounds. Much now depends on the owners of the dairy, I am keenly in favour of more industry in the countryside to help provide the money to keep it alive, but it must respect the setting.

Minsterley's brick church, completed in 1692, is a strange-looking building which seems younger than its age in style, yet the worn stone decorative work looks very old. In the church are several maidens' garlands, those wreaths of paper flowers and ribbons which were carried at the funerals of young girls and later hung in the church. The garlands at Minsterley date from between 1726 and 1794 and are now covered with plastic bags, but one has been brought down and put in a glass case where it can be seen. In most places this custom died out long ago, but at Abbots Ann in Hampshire it is still maintained and there garlands are hung for young men and girls of the parish who die before they marry and are of unblemished character.

Between this wild country and the Severn as it runs from the Welsh border to Shrewsbury there is a group of villages entirely different in character. First comes Ford along the Welshpool road, known to most local motorists for the Cross Gates Hotel which marks the turning for Vyrnwy, but which has much more to it than is seen by the main-road traveller. Turning off the road through a large modern development, one comes suddenly to the old village and, at the end, the steep valley of a brook with, perched high above on the skyline, a farm and a neat little church. Although much restored, this church still possesses hammerbeams in the chancel and some good carvings on the reredos. It is a pleasant surprise, but there were signs that this secret retreat was to be developed when I was last there.

Alberbury stands nearly on the border with Wales. Indeed it is said that when George IV as Prince of Wales stayed at Loton Park he walked over the border and picked a sprig off the first oak in Wales; and the Prince's Oak is still pointed out. Alberbury has a surprisingly large church for such an outlying position which must have been subjected to many raids in earlier days; remains of a castle by the church show the military importance of the site. The size of the church is explained by the monuments which show the presence of two great families, the Leightons of Loton Hall and the Lysters of Rowton Castle. One of these monuments to Sir Richard Lyster who died in 1691, was brought up from St. Chad's in Shrewsbury. The number of memorials from St. Chad's in other churches may appear puzzling, but it is a reminder of an incident which helped Telford to establish his reputation when he first came to the county. The wardens of the church had been worried by cracks in the fabric and asked Telford to investigate the matter and suggest a remedy. He told them that the trouble was much more serious than it appeared and that considerable work was needed. When this report was dismissed as being merely an effort to obtain a larger job than was necessary, Telford walked out of the meeting with the parting remark that they had better do something quickly or the church would fall down round their ears. A few days later early in the morning the building collapsed as forecast. Telford reported in a letter to a friend that it made a "very remarkable magnificent ruin".

Both the great houses at Alberbury have had chequered histories. Rowton Castle was destroyed by Llewellyn in 1482 and again in the Civil War, and later there was a Queen Anne brick house around which the present nineteenth-century 'castle' was built. Loton has been altered many times over the years and during the last war it was used as a gas dump by the army. The winding tracks which they made have since been used as a hill climb course.

Lady Leighton of the nineteenth century became famous for her miniature of the two Ladies of Llangollen, Lady Eleanor Butler and Miss Sara Ponsonby. They lived for fifty years together at Plas Newydd, Llangollen, and although they received many visitors they refused to have their portraits drawn, and it was only by a subterfuge that Lady Leighton was able to make her sketch. This was published after the death of the pair and was so popular that Lady Leighton was able to give £500 from the proceeds towards the cost of the tower of the little church at nearby Cardeston. There is a photograph of the engraving in the church which is a rather surprising place with green painted pews and a large not very good, modern wall painting showing Jesus coming to a group of people by the Jordan. It also has a barrel organ built in 1850, a rarity in a church; this is in quite good condition and was played for a service in 1968. The vicar tells me that he would like to obtain some rolls with modern hymn tunes so that the organ could be used more often. Cardeston's cottages and farms are so scattered that it hardly makes up as a village.

On the Welshpool road, the last village before the border is Wollaston which has acquired a certain fame because in its red brick church there is a brass plate in memory of "The Old, Old, very Old Man, Thomas Parr". Old Tom lived at Glyn cottage which was burnt down some years ago; I saw it on one of our early trips in the county, a little timber-framed thatched cottage. He was reputed to have been 152 years old when he died in 1635 as a result of being fêted in London where he had been taken. He claimed to have first married when he was eighty and to have married again at the age of 122. Modern writers discount his claims with science and statistics, but there are exceptions to most rules. I must confess that Tom's tale has a real Salopian ring of exaggeration about it; I can picture some of my acquaintances spinning just such a yarn. However, he is buried in Westminster Abbey and what greater seal could his claims require?

Westbury, on the Montgomery road, is quite a largish place for the area and is built on a square pattern of roads, which suggests a large-scale example of the plan frequently found in the smaller villages. The village shopkeeper has the broadest of Scottish accents which is strange to hear on this border. Yockleton is now just a mixture of old and new houses with the church standing away from the village over a little brook.

From this point, the Montgomery road avoïds the hills by running along the wide valley through which the Rea Brook flows. The first village is Worthen, a busy little settlement on a bend in the road, with a church which seems over-large and is very dark inside. The two-decker pulpit faces a goodly array of box pews, including the squire's with his crest on it, and in the centre are rows of medieval benches with open backs and bobbin ends which have an honest air of antiquity. The retention of these pews over the years cannot have been easy, for they do not look very comfortable and those using them must have felt very exposed compared with the occupants of the box pews.

Little Marton, by Marton Pool, is reputed to be an ancient settlement, but now it is merely a pleasant mixture of all types of houses on a bend in the road. It has a rather refreshing little Victorian church which draws attention to itself with a powder blue porch. Dr. Thomas Bray, born here in 1656, deserves to be better known than he is for he achieved much in his lifetime. After graduating at Oxford, he was appointed rector of Sheldon and became interested in the provision of parish libraries, a work which he continued when he was sent to Maryland. As a result of his efforts, by the time he died a number of libraries had been started in both England and America, and the Society for Promoting Christian Knowledge had been formed in 1698.

The last village before the border and Offa's Dyke, which here run together for several miles, is Chirbury, a meeting place of six roads. Now it is a dreamy place with the 'Herbert Arms', the church and black-and-white houses forming a group of which any village could be proud, while round the corner another group pose themselves to show that even without such important buildings a good effect can be achieved. Chirbury is another place which has been inhabited for a long time, the map showing two castle mounds and a motte and bailey nearby. The church has the sturdy tower which was regarded as essential for defensive purposes in this border area, but only dates from about 1300. Before that time there was a priory church, and although there have been many alterations, the rather grand appearance of the present church comes from the retention of the original proportions. The vicarage had an unusual private library of chained books left to the village in the seventeenth century by Lord Herbert of Cherbury, born at Eyton, but these are now in the County Archives.

Tiny Middleton-in-Chirbury nearby is equally ancient, for above it on Stapeley Hill is the Mitchell's Fold Stone Circle. Now only fifteen of the original number of about thirty stones are left and historians say that the circle was built in the Bronze Age about 1500 B.C. Local folk, however, know that there is a witch turned to stone and imprisoned in the circle. Legend has it that during a famine and drought a fairy gave the local people a cow which would provide each person with a pail of milk. The district witch knocked the bottom out of her bucket and fitted a sieve in its place so that although the cow tried to fill the bucket it failed and sank exhausted to the ground. The fairy came along just too late to save the cow, but she did root the witch to the ground inside the circle of stones.

This story is pictured on one of the pillars in the little Victorian church, where it was carved by the Reverend Waldegrave Brewster who went to the church in 1872. Unlike many scholars, he was deft with his hands and for thirty years he spent his spare time carving the wood and stone of the church. The pew ends which he started in 1877 and completed in 1890 have delightful portraits of parishoners of the time, which is a fitting tribute, for it is the people who make the villages.

3

North-west Shropshire—
Severn Valley and Border Hills

SHROPSHIRE is not an easy county to divide into areas for chapters owing to the fact that the roads radiate from Shrewsbury and do not follow the natural lie of the land. For some parts of the county an arrangement which ignored the roads might appear to be the most logical, but for those who like to know where the villages are as they read, it would be difficult to follow, and those who take the book as a travelling companion would find it less convenient. With these considerations in mind I have divided the northern half of the county into two chapters, roughly separated by the A49 road from Shrewsbury to Whitchurch, and the villages have been grouped around the main roads as far as possible.

Although this area has some high ground it is for the most part a plain with a large number of milk-producing farms; around Whitchurch in the north there have always been a number of cheese-makers, some of whom have a reputation for making the best Cheshire cheese.

This chapter deals with the north-western sector, beginning with the line of the Severn and sweeping round in a clockwise direction to the A49. The Upper Severn valley above Shrewsbury might be expected to be a rich area of riverside villages but in fact it is rather barren, for the Severn used to flood regularly and experience showed that it was safer to live on high ground well back from the river. The flooding problem has been fought for many years. Around Melverley there are embankments, locally known as 'argies', which were built in an early attempt to contain the waters. Of recent years an improvement has been made by smoothing the river banks to ease the flow, and in 1967 the Clywedog Dam was built above Llanidloes on a tributary of the Severn to control the water and further reduce the flood risk; 237 feet tall, this is the highest dam in Britain and has created a reservoir six miles long capable of holding 11,000 million gallons.

The first village from Shrewsbury along the A5 as it heads for North Wales is Bicton, which is fighting its own flood battle against the influx of new housing—and losing. Even the church which is not yet a hundred years old looks new and it seems that the village will eventually settle down as an outlying suburb of Shrewsbury.

At Montford the Severn is crossed by Telford's fine bridge, a well-known landmark. To cope with the increasing traffic on the A5 it was given a new road deck some years ago by removing the attractive red stone parapet, but the old arches are still able to carry the additional burden and withstand the river in flood, a fine tribute to the skill of the man whom the poet Southey called the 'Colossus of Roads'. An earlier bridge here had a deck of planks and it is said that the Sheriff removed some of these to make a gap to ambush Humphrey Kynaston, Shropshire's famous outlaw. Humphrey saw the danger in time and put his horse to the gap so that it was cleared successfully and he escaped. The letters H and K were cut in the turf on Knockin Heath to mark the length of the leap.

Fewer people see the village of Montford itself, which is a mile and half to the west. The old red stone church stands prominently above the lane with a fine view across to the hills. In the churchyard are buried Robert Darwin and his wife Susanah, the daughter of Josiah Wedgwood, who is famous for his china but should be equally remembered for his skill in organizing his factory and especially the labour relations in it. The couple were the parents of Charles Darwin, and Uncle Josiah Wedgwood's advice was largely responsible for his decision to accept the opportunity to go on that cruise of the *Beagle* which set him on the way to his later work.

Shrawardine has ventured quite close to the river, because here the land is higher. The defensive strength of the site attracted the early castle builders, but now there are only scant remains, as the castle was demolished after being besieged by the Parliamentarian forces in 1645 and the stones are said to have been used in buildings in Shrewsbury. The church suffered at the same time and has been largely rebuilt.

The way the riverside land has been avoided over the years is shown by the roundabout route necessary to get to Melverley which is by the Vyrnwy just before it joins the Severn. On my first trip there some years ago I found acres of land under water, but I felt rewarded for risking the perils of the floods as the little church high on the river's bank is a real gem, being one of the two wooden churches in the county. Glorious heavy timbers were used in building it and although it has been restored it retains its original simplicity. On my travels to bring memory up to date when I was preparing the material for this book, I met many people and received many suggestions as to places I should visit; Melverley folk would be delighted at the number of times I was told that their church was the one I should not miss. Among the village's few houses is the 'Tontine Inn'—which was presumably originally built out of the proceeds of a tontine, a fund to which a group of men subscribed, the money going to the last survivor. This was a favourite form of 'insurance' among the river men of the Severn. The dangers of floods in this area are well illustrated by a tale told locally that after a sudden flood caused by a cloudburst in the Welsh Hills, a labourer who had fallen asleep on a haycock was swept away and did not wake till his strange craft reached Montford Bridge. This is so similar to stories told in other parts of the country that it may well be part of English folklore.

The lanes in this area are maze-like and the signposting typically Salopian, but Nesscliff Hill makes a good point to steer by. A flight of rough steps lead up its steep slopes to the cave,

Telford's Montford Bridge has been given a new deck

Test bridge built at Longdon upon Tern by Telford

Tools made by Mr Higgs Snr. for shaping rail ends

Percy Hopcraft's thatching leggatt studded with horseshoe nails

The 'old work' at Viroconium

Peace has returned to Tong

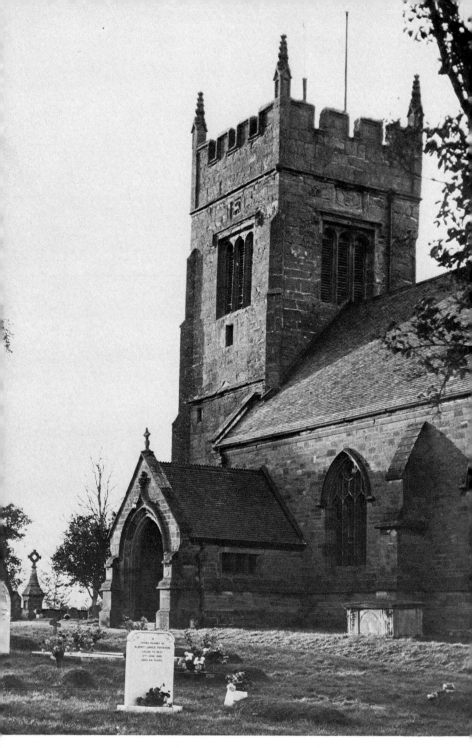

The tower at Sutton Maddock

which is claimed to have been the hide-out of Humphrey Kynaston, Shropshire's outlaw. This has two compartments, one for Humphrey and one for his horse. Unlike Robin Hood and most other outlaws, Humphrey is quite well documented. He was born in 1470, the youngest son of Sir Roger Kynaston of Hordley, and in 1491 he became keeper of Myddle Castle, but so neglected this duty that the castle fell into ruins. As a result of his association with bad company Humphrey was soon heavily in debt and eventually he was concerned with several others in a murder which led to his being outlawed. He kept in favour with the poor of the district in the traditional way by sharing the spoils of his robberies with them and this no doubt helped him to escape capture. For some unknown reason he was pardoned in 1516, after which he went to live peacefully on a small property which he owned at Welshpool. The Kynaston family still has the pardon document.

Nowadays Nesscliff is a most law-abiding place with quite a lot of new buildings, including a modern school. The previous building with its school house has been taken over by two Shrewsbury teachers, David and Jackie Brown, who saw the potential of the old school rooms as an art studio. They held their first exhibition in April 1971 and now hold five events a year showing paintings, pottery, sculpture and graphics. The aim is to provide an opportunity for professional artists to put their work before the public and the couple are content if the venture does no more than pay its way. There is a pleasant reminder of the previous use of the building in a notice asking visitors to knock first, then if no reply is received to pull a chain gently. This tolls the old school bell which has a delightful note. No doubt they are encouraged in their venture by the verse high up on the wall: "God prosper and prolong this public good; A school erected where a chapel stood."

My pilgrimage round the villages of these two counties was at times a sobering enterprise, for in some places the past has been erased so cleanly that now there is no sign of it. Knockin is an example. There is a pleasantly wide street with neat houses and a heavily restored church. Behind this is a garden covering the site of Knockin Castle to which at the very beginning of the thirteenth

D

century John le Strange had brought home his new bride, the widowed queen of Cyprus. By the sixteenth century Leland noted that the building was in ruins; and now Knockin seems far too modest a place to have ever had a castle.

At nearby Kinnerley the church standing up on the bend of the road above the houses and built of the seemingly inexhaustible supply of local red stone has such a fortress-like appearance that it suggests a castle.

The border between England and Wales cuts through the 'Lion Hotel' in Llanymynech which lies in typical flat border country and is dominated by Llanymynech Hill, a landmark used by Offa in sighting the line of his Dyke. Prominent along the very wide main street which makes the village seem more important than it is, stands the church, which was built in 1845 in Norman style, a plan carried through with such skill and thoroughness that the result is more interesting than it sounds. Yet Llanymynech has no need for such mock antiquity for it has real history in the great hill above it, which was mined by the Romans for copper, lead and zinc. In 1965 a party of schoolboys exploring the largest of the old workings Ogof's Hole, a few hundred yards from the golf course, found a hoard of silver Roman denarii. Local legend has supplied several alternative explanations of this hole: it has been said to be the entrance to Fairyland; or part of a secret passage leading to the vanished Carreghofa Castle; while a blind fiddler and a harpist are reputed to have lost their ways in the tunnels, and there are people who claim to have heard the music of these departed players.

Another Welsh-sounding place now on the Shropshire side of the border is Llanyblodwel. Every time I have been there it has been raining. Reason suggests that this is sheer coincidence, but Llanyblodwel is one of those hidden-in-the-hills places which seem to attract rain. Hidden in the hills it certainly is, for it is reached by a devious road that goes down into the Tanat valley and it is so tucked away that parts of it can easily be missed. It is well worth seeking out and exploring. Down by the river is the bridge and an inn well-known to fishermen, making an enchanting corner that in spirit belongs to Wales rather than to England. Another road which the casual traveller could well overlook, leads to the church which is so unusual that it merits a special visit.

Little is known about its beginnings, but it is mentioned as being transferred in 1160, and Norman features in the south doorway indicate an early date. As it stands the church is a striking monument to John Parker, Vicar of Llanyblodwel from 1845 to 1860. When he went to the parish the south wall of the church was in a dangerous state and much other work was needed. Some people might have been discouraged by the state of the building or attempted some minor repairs to stave off complete collapse, but John Parker tackled problem after problem and transformed the church. The little community appears to have been completely dominated by the fierce enthusiasm of their new incumbent, who spent £10,000 on the church. The small bellcote was replaced by a new octagonal tower with a slightly bowed stone spire, which is almost detached from the main body of the church. The junction has an arch bearing the inscription, "From thunder and lightning, earthquake and flood, good Lord deliver us." The interior of the church shows the full glory of John Parker's imaginative genius with painted decorations on the arches of the arcade and over the windows, and large panels of texts. The plentiful use of rich hues and gold leaf creates a riot of colour, making a church which is quite unique. It is not to everyone's taste, indeed part of the work was later covered up with flat colour wash. In 1958–60 this covering was removed to show again the full effect of John Parker's work and this must be one of the rare cases where a nineteenth-century restoration has itself been restored. Such a church would be unusual anywhere; in the wooded Tanat valley by the Welsh border it comes as a shock.

West Felton is another village that does not reveal its true self to the hurrying traveller, who sees only a collection of houses and filling stations just south of Oswestry; the old village lies a mile to the west at a wooded junction of lanes and is comfortingly snug after the bleak main road. Nearby at Woolston is the Holy Well of St. Winifred. She lived in the seventh century and

planned to devote her life to the church. A local prince had other
ideas and when he was rejected he drew out his sword and cut off
Winifred's head, which fell to the ground. Immediately a spring
came up and engulfed the prince; the waters were later found to
be of great purity and St. Winifred's Well at Holywell in Flint,
as it became known, was a place of pilgrimage for centuries. Fortunately Winifred's uncle, Bueno, was near at hand and he replaced the saint's head which, in answer to his prayers, was joined
to her body with only a thin line showing round her neck. When,
after a good life, she died, she was buried at Gwytherin in Den-
bighshire. In the reign of King Stephen, when the holy bones were
being taken to the Abbey Church in Shrewsbury, the procession
stopped at Woolston and here another spring appeared. This is
covered by a timber-framed building and was also a place of
pilgrimage.

Along the border of the county facing Denbigh are Whittington, Selattyn and St. Martin's, Whittington is known to drivers
along the A5 for the awkward bends in the road at its approach
and for the main street where the two round towers of the gatehouse of the old castle make a pleasing picture; few of those who
stop to look at the ducks posing in the moat realize that the
towers have been lived in for many years.

This was an important defensive position in the past for it
commanded one of the few routes through the vast area of marshland that then covered the district. It was the flowers of the
cottongrass which grew on this that earned the settlement its
name of White Town. After the Norman invasion, Pain Peverel,
founder of the Peverel of the Peak family, held the castle at one
time, but it was not until 1221 that the Fitz-Warines built the
stone castle, parts of which can still be seen now. This Fitz-
Warine connection is put forward as evidence to support the claim
that Dick Whittington was a local boy who made good, for it will
be remembered that when the pantomime hero got to London his
first job was with a merchant named Fitzwarren who, it is suggested, could have been a member of a branch of the local family.
Not content with claiming one pantomime, the people of the

district also point out that the name Babbins Wood nearby could be a corruption of Baban's Wood, and since Baban is Welsh for baby this could have been the site of the incidents in *The Babes in the Wood*.

The church at Whittington has its own connections which are so deep-rooted that they too are almost 'trad'. A panel behind the choir stalls records the fact that William Walsham How was rector at the church for twenty-eight years. He left to take an appointment in London where he was known as the Children's Bishop for his work for young people, and a later move took him to Wakefield. But to many people he is best known for the hymns which he wrote including 'Summer suns are glowing'.

Halston nearby, was the home of Jack Mytton who brightened the early years of the nineteenth century with the activities which earned him his place as Shropshire's eccentric. Eccentric he certainly was, but less is heard of the fact that he was also a champion farmer who one year won every prize for clean grain fields at the Shropshire Agricultural Meeting except one, and that was a field of barley which was found to contain wild oats, a result which probably delighted his twisted sense of humour. As a horseman also, Jack Mytton was outstanding. In order to hunt with a Staffordshire pack of hounds he would regularly ride across the county in the morning and then return again after the meeting. His exploits have become almost part of Shropshire folklore and although they may have been embroidered in the course of time they indicate that he was utterly fearless. Typical was the occasion when a friend protested at the rate at which he was driving a horse and gig. Mytton solicitously asked if he had been hurt in being upset in a gig. His friend replied that fortunately he had escaped that. "Well you have now," retorted Mytton, as he put the wheel of the gig up the bank and tipped it over. On another occasion he drove a horse and gig over a ha-ha ditch for a wager. He would go shooting wildfowl in a light jacket and white linen trousers; and when a man in a coffee shop talked too much he put a burning coal in the man's pocket so that he stopped and dashed out to jump in a horse trough.

Such brilliant living could not last for long and by the time he was thirty-eight his money had run out and he died in the King's Bench prison. Halston's church in the grounds of Mytton's old home is a timber-framed building rather grander than the one at Melverley with a fine array of box pews and hatchments.

Selattyn is a sterner place with the line of Offa's Dyke going over its hill on which there is an ancient British camp and a tower set up last century in honour of Gwen, a warrior killed in a battle between Britons and Saxons. It is an ups-downy place where the road is above the church so that you look down on it, as at St. David's in South Wales.

St. Martin's, almost the most north-westerly point of the county, is growing rapidly in an ungainly sort of way but there is still a glimpse of the old village at the top of the bank where church and almshouses stand together. The almshouses have in fact changed, although the work has been done so skilfully that it is not apparent. The old dormer windows have been removed and the block converted into old people's homes so that it still serves a useful purpose. The church has a Welsh atmosphere inside with its sombre dark box pews which still have brass name-plates on them. There is also a Welshness about the squire's simple square pew—none of the horse-box nonsense there, although the vicar told me that he thought there had been curtains round it at one time. Standing foursquare against the south wall is the three-decker pulpit, again very forthright and commanding, although the gallery which is usually to be found with this style of pulpit has been removed as it was affected by dry rot.

Only three miles away, Duddleston is an upstart place for this countrysider, for it largely originated in the eighteenth century when many cottages were built by squatters on the then unenclosed Duddleston Heath. This has given it a scattered nature. The church is a late-comer too, being mainly nineteenth century with an octagonal tower and a spire. But in the autumn sunlight it looked as well settled as others in the countryside and it has obviously been well-loved over the years for it has a table of gifts in the chancel which unusually records the gift of a clock in 1866.

The Ellesmere countryside has a number of meres which are becoming increasingly popular among fishermen and small boat sailors, but they belong elsewhere as does Ellesmere itself, for this is an ancient market town. Welshampton, a few miles east, is near the border with that detached island of Flintshire that is puzzlingly known as Maelor-of-the-Saxons. In fact this land passed to Wales as the dowry of a Saxon lady who married a Welshman, an indication that not all the early contacts between the two nations were war-like. Welshampton itself was formerly on the Welsh side of the border, but now it looks very English at is sits neatly by the A495 road between Ellesmere and Whitchurch. It has a nineteenth-century church which looks rather too grand for the little bell-cote over it; and it is a strange place to see a window to Mosheshue, a Basuto Chief's son, who died there in 1863 while studying. This is one of those finds which start one musing, for although it is only just over a hundred years ago since Mosheshue came to the district it must have seemed a tremendous venture at the time.

In the V-shaped sector between the A5 road going to Wales and the A49 road to Whitchurch and the north there is a plain with a maze of little roads and many small villages. The northern part is particularly low-lying with hump-backed bridges over streams and canals.

Shrewsbury is spreading outwards rapidly, and fields where I helped to gather potatoes only fifteen years ago are now covered with houses. But Berwick down by the river is still quiet with the great house standing in its pleasant grounds and looking rather too stately for the Shropshire most people think of.

At Battlefield, near the junction where the Market Drayton road branches off the Whitchurch road, is the church, which is all that remains of the college established by Henry IV as a chantry college to pray for the souls of those slain in the Battle of Shrewsbury in 1406. By the eighteenth century the church had fallen into disrepair and in the following century it was thoroughly restored, but it still retains its original grand proportions. Round the beams are reproductions of the shields of the king and his knights, and the church has a monument, with four arches like an Easter

Sepulchre, to John Corbet who died in 1817 and whose daughter restored the building.

To the west are Fitz, Great Ness and Little Ness. Fitz looks a typical hidden-away-in-the-woods place, yet it is within a quarter of a mile of the banks of the Severn. It is an oasis of peace with brick houses and weatherboarded barns which must have seemed very desirable to Thomas Pyton 'late a merchant in America' who was buried there in 1781. In the gallery of the brick church is a barrel organ which was used for providing music at one time. In 1966 the rector gave me a demonstration of it and it burst into tune immediately he began turning the handle. The Reverend Waldegrave Brewster who did so much carving in Middleton moved here in 1901 and did further work, but in a more restrained style.

In Great Ness the local red stone was used to build the church, which has a fine old door bearing the date 1618. Inside there is one of those pleasing links of continuity which are so delightful to find; for the coat of arms bears a note that it was given by the two churchwardens in 1800 and restored by its churchwardens in 1956. Little Ness is another place where the local red stone and rich red brick give a rosy glow to the village. Brick is sometimes regarded as an inferior building material, but these villages show that properly used it can produce a very comfortable appearance.

Baschurch is growing into quite a sizeable place with many new houses, but as usual the nucleus is by the church which is quite large and has been much renewed. The work in 1790 was undertaken by Thomas Telford who had come up to the county in 1786 to do repairs to Shrewsbury Castle for William Pulteney. In the following year he became Surveyor of Public Works for the County of Salop and he later estimated that between 1790 and 1796 he had been responsible for building no less than forty road bridges. This church restoration was only one of many similar jobs which he managed to cope with at the time he was starting his new career and is evidence of the immense energy which he showed throughout his life.

It was at Boreatton nearby that Dame Agnes Hunt first opened her hospital in a collection of huts. When further expansion became impossible on the site it was necessary to move to Oswestry where, as the Robert Jones and Agnes Hunt Orthopaedic Hospital, it has become the largest of its kind in the western world.

Visitors to the area are always amused by the signposts to Ruyton-XI-Towns, which must be one of the earliest examples of local government 'take-overs', for it was in the twelfth century that eleven towns were joined into one. With such a promising start it might be expected that Ruyton would have grown into a considerable town, but although it stretches along the road for over a mile from the neat little round house by the bridge over the Perry, it remains an inconsequential place. At the highest point is the church and the remains of the castle built by the Earl of Arundel in the fourteenth century. Ruyton still has a 'castle', for just outside the village is Ruyton Manor, a building of 1860 complete with a crenellated tower and terraced garden.

There is another nineteenth-century 'ancient building' at Albrighton on the Whitchurch road, for what appears to be a little Norman church perched rather precariously above a bend in the road was built in 1840. Nowadays traffic rushes through and most people remember Albrighton for the high walls of the Hall which is now the Royal Normal College for the Blind. For me it has a more modern memory, for it was in the little village shop that I made my first transaction with the new decimal coinage.

Further along the road Preston Gubbals preserves some peace because much of the village lies with the church away from the main road. At Harmerhill there are some houses with rooms cut back into the rock of the hill behind them. Mrs. Williams of Newtown told me that her uncle lived in one of these for many years and had used the 'rock room' as a workshop.

Myddle lies down the side of a hill away from the A528 and is built across a wide valley, with the newer building near the main road and a delightful looking old inn with very decorative chimneys at the bottom of the slope. The road then climbs up to the older houses and the church which, despite being rebuilt and twice restored, still retains a number of memorials to early

Atcherleys. Only a circular stair turret remains of the fourteenth-century castle which the outlaw Humphrey Kynaston allowed to deteriorate. In the seventeenth century another member of the family was more responsible, for when the church tower needed rebuilding he offered to do this as far as his own height if the village would do the rest. This could be a useful example for modern vicars organizing appeals for funds for such work!

Shade Oak, a seventeenth-century brick house at Cockshutt, has been painted black and white to match the local pattern. Parts of the timber-framed Wycherley Hall have also been replaced with black-and-white painted brickwork. This type of deception has now been practised over so many years in the county that it can almost be counted as an ancient custom and accepted by all but the strictest purists.

At Hordley, tucked away in the lanes, the past is gradually being lost, the Shropshire Union Canal is dry, and in a farmhouse are the remains of the old home of the Kynastons.

Over towards the north-east of the county the land becomes drier and as a result there are larger villages and a number of estates. Hadnall, a main road village, has suffered over the years. Now an excellent road lets the traffic speed through, but getting rid of the cars so quickly endangers life and is not the best answer for the peace of a village. It is a pity that General Viscount Hill was not available to help defend the villagers' interests. Born at Prees Hall, he fought in the Peninsula War and continued to serve under Wellington up to Waterloo. He is buried in the much restored church and there is a monument to him there which has as mourners a shepherd and a guardsman to represent the two sides of his life. This is not as well known as his column in Shrewsbury, which stands 133 ft. 6 in. tall; the 17-ft. concrete figure of Lord Hill topping what is claimed to be the largest Doric column in the world.

Grinshill and Clive lying back from the road are much more peaceful places. Above Grinshill are the quarries where stone for local building has been taken since Roman times. However, this activity does not appear to have affected the village which has a delightful street along the bottom of the valley. The church is up a turning and does not seem to be in keeping with the village, although it is built of local stone. Perhaps this is because it dates only from the nineteenth century and has not had time to settle down yet. The garish front of the 'Elephant and Castle' Hotel is also a strange sight in such a quiet village; the name and sign are the crest of the Corbets.

On the hill above Grinshill is Clive which is cosy and respectable even when the rain sweeps across the wide view of Shropshire seen from the churchyard. Although there has been a church at Clive since the twelfth century, the present structure was largely built in Victorian days and looks it, but is none the worse for that as it fits in well with the big houses of the village. Clive Hall, an Elizabethan house which has been extended over the years, was the birthplace in 1640 of William Wycherley, the Restoration dramatist, a larger than life character who could have stepped out of a play himself. His first work *Love in a Wood* was an immediate success and he followed this with other comedies which were cleverly constructed with amusing situations and had that streak of indecency which was demanded of dramatists of that era. Despite his success he was rarely out of debt and constantly in trouble.

Loppington, to the west of Wem, is a sleepy place with brick and timber-framed houses mingling nicely along wide streets which I have always found empty, yet in the past they had noisy enough scenes. Outside the 'Dickins Arms', in the middle of the road, is what is claimed to be the only surviving ring for tethering bulls for baiting in the county. It is thought to have last been in use about 1835 when the practice was banned. One villager I met told me that he remembered that at one time it was said that if you turned the ring over you claimed to be the best man in Loppington and ready to meet any challengers. Certainly the villagers take a great deal of pride in the ring and if it is covered when road work is done they make sure that it is pecked out again immediately. Loppington has recently taken an interest in its past and has found remnants of its cattle pound; there is also a plan to replace the stocks. The church is nicely set back down a side road. Usually, it is the older monuments in churches which attract attention, but at Loppington there is a striking modern memorial to William Vaughan, Vicar 1935–40, with a figure in a clerical gown holding a flaming sword in one hand and scales in the other —the whole a complicated and highly coloured design.

Often I find that it is atmosphere not size that creates the most attractive villages. Loppington, for instance is larger than Newtown, but it seems to have more of the feel of a village. Newtown has some attractive cottages and farmhouses but, perhaps because it is so tidy, it has an urban air. The Victorian church is dedicated to King Charles the Martyr and displays some framed prints of the King's execution and burial—unusual sights in a church.

In the country to the north of Wem, around Whixall, there are stretches of peat bogs, desolate places from which peat is still cut, although it is now used more for agricultural and horticultural purposes than for fuel as in the old days. The peat bogs are not places of beauty and the workings look even less attractive for they contain a high percentage of water, making conditions most unpleasant. Before the peat can be reached the topsoil has to be removed. Trenches are then dug and the peat cut out in blocks or turves which are laid in rows to dry. When the surplus moisture has drained off, the turves are built into cone-shaped mounds with spaces left to allow the air to circulate and dry them. Draining schemes are now enabling much of the workings to be reclaimed for agricultural use.

I shall not forget Edstaston quickly, for as I went into the church I was greeted by the strains of the Wedding March; it is not very often that one walks down the aisle to this music! The village is only a tiny place with a few houses where weddings must be rare, so I could well understand that the organist felt that he was in need of practice.

Prees is another of those places which seem to be just a flash of new development to the main-road driver but, as so often is the case, along the side streets it shows its real character, especially up the hill towards the church and Prees Hall, where General

Viscount Hill was born. In the church there is a striking memorial to his father, Sir John Hill, which shows his funeral procession. Another of the many memorials to members of the family is to Lieutenant-Colonel Hill, who died in 1885 from a fall at Mount Pilatus, Lucerne. What tales there are in the memorials in churches—any fiction writer seeking ideas for a plot could find enough inspiration in them to give full rein to his imagination.

And so to Lee Brockhurst where I was greeted by the squealing of what sounded like ten thousand young pigs being massacred, but was probably feeding time, for the noise quickly subsided. Then all was peace. In contrast to Prees, Lee Brockhurst is scattered along a curling wooded lane with a little Norman church which is all modesty. It makes you think of primroses, violets and all that is the English countryside.

4

North-east Shropshire—
The Civilized Countryside

THIS chapter covers the north-eastern section of Shropshire, from the A5113 which runs from Shrewsbury to Whitchurch, round to the Severn valley east of Shrewsbury. It is an area which contains—unusually for the county—several large estates, the rich agricultural region around Market Drayton, and the industrial district verging on the West Midlands which includes the area above the Severn Gorge that has become Telford New Town. From Shawbury, which is on the western edge of the region, an arc of fifteen miles radius covers the whole area, but although it is small in size the countryside is very varied. Some forty years ago I took a cousin who had just returned from Canada for some cycle trips through Cheshire and into this part of Shropshire and I still remember his constant surprise at the ever-changing scenery. He had been in a country where the view from a train window was the same for hours on end; here every few minutes on a bicycle brought new delights. Despite the march of time, Shropshire scenery still has that variety; it is as if it were composed of a myriad of separate particles rather than being an homogeneous mass. Each district keeps its individuality and there is little of the 'bleeding' of atmosphere in the way that colours run together in water-colour painting.

Shawbury is perhaps not the best starting point because a large R.A.F. training establishment, which includes a Meteorological Office station, has been established there and as a result, especially of recent years, the village is becoming urbanized. We may have benefited by having the weather men on the doorstep so that a quick telephone call will get us an 'instant' forecast for the next few hours—which is very useful, especially when trying to decide if it is worth setting out with a camera—but Shawbury has suffered an invasion of its airspace by screaming planes and its streets are becoming modernized out of recognition. As so often happens, round by the church it is still possible to see what the village might have been like. Here stand some timber-framed houses and the red brick Georgian 'Elephant and Castle Hotel'. The church is so wide inside that it appears cavernous, with a splash of colour on the ornate carved and painted reredos, the work of a nineteenth-century lady of the Corbet family.

The real place to see the Corbets is Moreton Corbet, a mile and a half away. Now it is another of the typically modest villages of the county with cottages set along a lane which Moreton Corbet Castle dominates, even though it is now a ruin. The Corbets had lived there since the early thirteenth century when the stone Keep was built. The full flowering of the building came in 1579 when Sir Richard Corbet added a magnificent house to the east and south sides of the castle. At the time of the Civil War this great residence was naturally fortified against the Parliamentarians who besieged it in 1644 and later burnt it down. Fortunately the shell survived and even today this is sufficiently complete to indicate that it would have been one of the outstanding houses of the country if it had not been destroyed. The walls now stand as a haunting reminder of what might have been, and are all the more impressive because they are set starkly in open ground. Beside it is the perfect group of the half-timbered rectory and the church standing behind a green in a churchyard approached by a tree-lined drive. In the church are a fine collection of Corbet memorials, many with figures on tomb chests, some of which are coloured, and many representations of their elephant and castle crest. It is an impressive tribute to the wealth and importance of the family.

Stanton upon Hine Heath is in complete contrast, for it is a place of large, red brick houses and a modest little church standing on a hillock at the end of the village with a wide view to the west from the porch. Stanton is a delightfully rural place where Mary Webb lived from the time she was about twelve until she was twenty-one. It was an ideal situation for her to develop that awareness of the countryside which led eventually to her writing the novels which have continued to sell over the years, although during her lifetime the author complained to her publisher that she had to live on 'bread and scrape'.

North along the Market Drayton road is Hodnet, one of the few places that have been able to retain their characters despite the handicap of being on a main road. I never drive into the village without marvelling at the fact that although it has a busy road junction at its focal point it still looks so inviting. Perhaps this is due to the rise of the road to the corner by the church, which is posed perfectly for viewing. Hodnet has been the home of great families for centuries with the Hills, the Vernons and then the Hebers, who perhaps brought it the most fame. Richard Heber, of the eighteenth century, had one of the largest collections of books in the country and was founder member of the Athenaeum Club. His brother Henry became a bishop and is remembered especially for his hymn-writing which included that favourite 'From Greenland's Icy Mountains'. There is a portrait of the bishop by Chantrey in the church, which also has memorials of the other families who owned the estate. An interesting curio is a case of chained books which includes a breeches Bible, a Bible dated 1613 printed by Robert Barker, and a manuscript missal on which the colours stand out like jewels. The present Hall replaced the earlier house in 1870. The grounds are visited every year by many thousands of people who come to see the gardens, which were created by the late Brigadier Heber Percy, and which give a wonderful show for most of the year, but are especially beautiful in the spring when the daffodils are in bloom round the lake.

Hodnet's neighbouring park, Hawkstone, created by the Hills, is even more famous and was one of the first of the stately homes run as a 'business'. Great houses had by tradition been open to visitors, but such visits had been free, except for the expected

Flounder's Folly above Westhope

A modern shepherd in the
Vaughan window at Clungunford

The Cantlin stone and cross
on the lonely Clun Forest

The stables at Shipton, with the dovecote behind

Upton Magna gathers around its green

tips to the servants. The estate at Hawkstone is believed to have been the first opened for a fee, and a copy of a guide-book dated 1776 still exists. Sir Richard Hill, the second baronet, was very keen on the project, and the attractions in his time included a grotto, a hermitage with a hermit, an artificial ruin and other features which even impressed Dr. Johnson who was not the most susceptible of travellers. Like some of his modern counterparts, Sir Richard introduced new features from time to time to maintain interest.

On the west of Hawkstone Park is Weston, a rather delightful place, where trees and houses pour down the hillside from the church, outside of which some very dilapidated stocks are preserved.

This north-eastern corner of the county always appears to be surprisingly civilized to me because I have lived in the south of the county where most of the villages have a rural disorder. In this area they are neater with larger houses arranged in a more orderly fashion. Moreton Say is typical, very neat and well-kept; and when I was there last the vicarage was being prepared for a new incumbent after a spell without one. In these days, when so many villages are losing their vicars, this is a rare occurrence. The church is one of those fascinating jigsaws which please those with architectural interests, for while the outside is largely eighteenth-century brick, this is a shell built outside the original thirteenth-century stone building, parts of which remain in the interior. Thus for those who like looking for the structural history of buildings there are plenty of clues. There is also a most unusual memorial which shows Jane Vernon between her two husbands John Bostock of Moreton Say and Sir Richard Grosvenor of Eccleston. This was erected in 1623, and as Lady Jane lived for a further twenty-five years she no doubt looked many times at her strange memorial which attracts more attention than that of Robert Clive, who was baptized in the church in 1725 and buried there in 1774 as Baron Clive. The family home of Styche Hall midway to Market Drayton is a whitewashed brick house which was rebuilt in Clive's time. The story of Clive's rise to fame

E

and power was one of the inspiring episodes of the history books of my schooldays, but since then historians have become franker and as one learns of the ways in which he acquired the wealth that refounded the family fortunes, one can only visualize the newspaper headlines that would nowadays follow a parliamentary inquiry into such actions. At the time they only produced a resolution that he had rendered "great and meritorious services to his country".

The difference between this area and the rest of the county is again brought out vividly at Calverhall which is so neat and tidy that it appears to be a modern village, yet next to the church is a row of almshouses dated 1724. The block is shorter than it used to be because when the church was rebuilt in the nineteenth century the end of the almshouses was knocked down to allow for the extension of the south aisle of the church. Another reminder of the village's past is in the name of the village inn, 'The Old Jack', for this refers to the Jack of Corra, a leather bottle from which at one time any traveller passing through the village could drink beer on payment of one penny; the old bottle is pictured on the inn sign. Corra is an old version of the village name; a further variant is Cloverley, which is found at Cloverley Hall, now a conference centre.

Ightfield, a mile and a half away, is another village of red brick houses, but it is a little less prim than Calverhall. The church stands with the school away from the village on a knoll. It has a good brass to Dame Margaret Calverley and another to her father "the good William Maynwaring". A later member of this family, Arthur Mainwaring, won fame with his first poem 'Tarquin and Tullia' which was a satire on William and Mary. Later he brought out *The Medley* as a rival to *The Examiner*. This was highly thought of by Jonathan Swift. He is also said to have helped Steele during his early days and the first number of *The Tatler* was dedicated to him.

The road to Adderley passes through the grounds of Shavington Hall and Adderley Hall, which were the respective homes of the Kilmoreys and the Corbets who waged a feud over their rights in the village church. Now their chapels and their monuments are out of sight, for since 1956 these, with the chancel, have been boarded off "to fit the needs of a smaller parish". The effect is disturbing, for the partition has the appearance of a temporary affair and gives the impression that repairs are being carried out. Meanwhile dust and neglect is settling on the fine screen and the monuments. No doubt this is a very practical solution, but it is a great pity that a better arrangement could not have been made.

In the far north-east of the county is Norton in Hales which, when I last saw it, had a plaque awarded for being the best-kept village in Shropshire on its little green beside an unsightly notice warning of traffic restrictions (when will the planners control their own highway departments?) and the Bradling Stone. This is a great stone on which, it is said, the villagers used to bump anyone found working after midday on Shrove Tuesday. The church was rebuilt in the nineteenth century and its most striking feature is the alabaster monument to Sir Rowland Cotton and his wife (who died in childbirth) which is now in the porch. It is a most impressive piece of work with decorated columns, and shows Sir Rowland in ornamental armour and his wife with her breasts bared and her daughter in her arms.

Market Drayton is too large and busy to be considered as a village, but no account of the villages of the county would be complete without mention of the work done by E. G. Webb and A. Jackson who were the organizers for the Cheshire and Shropshire branch of the Rural Industries Bureau (later renamed The Council for Small Industries in Rural Areas) based in Market Drayton. Working with a very small organization, these two enthusiasts did a great deal for the villages of the area by helping the craftsmen to meet the demands of modern times. Some years ago the Rural Industries Bureau was indentified by many people as being an organization for 'Ye Olde Craftsmenne' and this eager couple did everything to foster a more up-to-date picture of its activities. If I approached them for the name of a good 'old-fashioned' smith or carpenter, they would argue for half an hour threatening, jocularly, to throw me down the office stairs; then they would casually give me the address I wanted and add another lecture about the need to create a better image of village craftsmen.

Luckily for our relations, I was able to place a number of articles on the way in which craftsmen had coped with changing conditions. For this material I received willing co-operation, and was introduced to saddle-makers in small villages who were exporting their products overseas; a furniture-maker turned restorer after a course, who was doing work for National Trust properties and in other great houses; and a number of smiths and small engineers who had been able to grow into quite reasonably sized firms because of the advice and opportunities which the Bureau brought them. Craftsmen are prickly people at times, but this pair certainly had the art of securing their co-operation.

South from Market Drayton, there is a chain of places which are on the borders of Staffordshire in rich, often park-like country. Cheswardine, where the rebuilt church is in the middle of the T-shaped village, is a centre for the Milk Marketing Board AI Service, another organization which has done much to help the countryside over recent years. In 1949 when I went on a farm as a trainee as part of my effort to learn more about the countryside, nearly every farm kept its own bull. Handling old Jasper, our Friesian bull, was a task which demanded that you kept your wits about you. I well remember the day his tether broke loose and we had to carry out repairs while he tucked into an extra ration of oats put in his manger as a bribe. The farm had a herd of Friesians and we thought we were being rather daring in calling in the 'bull with the bowler hat', as the AI inseminator was then known, to serve the one little Jersey heifer which was kept. Nowadays the position is reversed. Figures tell the story: in 1944 when the first Milk Marketing Board centre came into operation at Beccles, 2,600 inseminations were completed; in 1972/73 there were twenty-three main centres and sixty-seven sub-centres of the M.M.B. in England and Wales and the number of inseminations totalled over two million. The service not only relieves the farmer of the difficulties and expense of keeping a bull, but more importantly, also enables him to have the use of some of the best animals in the various breeds, so that over the years there has been an improvement in the type of animals on our farms and increased milk production.

I am used to the confined valleys of the west so this open countryside of the eastern edge of the county always seems strange to me and when I get on to one of the main roads, like the A41 at Hinstock, and encounter modern traffic conditions, I do feel really very far from home. The old church here towers over the houses from a striking position high up on an island site surrounded by four roads.

At Stoke upon Tern, a few miles west, things are quieter. The Victorian looking village of red brick houses gazes out from a small rise across the wide valley of the Tern, where the striking black-and-white Petsey House and the church stand out. The church was rebuilt in the nineteenth century but has retained one of those imposing Corbet memorials that are so frequently found in the county—this one is to the sixteenth-century Sir Reginald Corbet, Justice of the King's Bench, and serves as a reminder that the first home of the Corbets in the county was a castle nearby, although little trace of this can now be seen.

Much of Child's Ercall lies round a large, walled field, which looks as if it might have been the village common at one time. The church stands at the top to complete what would have been quite a pleasant picture if only the pole planters had run their overhead wires somewhere else.

A road running parallel to one of the runways of a vast disused airfield leads to Great Bolas, or Bolas Magna as the parish is called. It has an appealing disorderliness, like a traditional country girl with the wind in her hair. There is a pretty little bridge at the approach to the village and a charming street of varied cottages with the school and the church tucked away in a corner. Great Bolas has some fascinating names associated with it. The eighteenth-century nave and tower of the church were designed by John Willdig; in the church there are many memorials to the Oggles; and there was Sarah Hoggins, the miller's daughter. I cannot understand why there should have been an attempt to claim the story of Dick Whittington for the county when there is the true life story of Sarah Hoggins, who was as beautiful as she deserved to be with a plain name like that. Into Bolas Magna, as it was then called, came the handsome but sad-faced Harry. Like all the best stories from the past there are several versions of what happened in the next few months—some say that he was so smitten by Sarah's beauty that he obtained a job with the miller, others that Sarah lost her heart to the pathetic stranger and took pity on him—but woo they did and later wed at St. Mildred's church in Bread Street, London, which must have seemed strange to the local folk, who would have expected to see the show at their own little church. Afterwards the couple lived at Bolas in a modest house till one day a message came for Harry. He read this and then went on several secret trips, which revived some of the early rumours that he was connected with highwaymen or smugglers, but on his return he suggested to Sarah that they went off together on a holiday trip to see the country. In the course of this they passed Burghley House near Stamford in Lincolnshire and Harry asked his wife if she liked it. Sarah replied that she thought it was a very splendid house and Harry then told her that she should be mistress of it, for he was now the Earl of Exeter. Unfortunately, Sarah did not enjoy her new estate for very long for she died in 1797. Tennyson wrote a poem based on the story of Sarah, in which Harry is cast as a painter.

Those who think of Shropshire as a black-and-white county should surely visit this part of it, especially in the autumn when the rich brown and gold of the trees combines with the red stone and red brick of which so many of the buildings are built, to bring out a warmth in the villages which is too little known. The new image may not fit preconceived ideas of the county but it will come as a delightfully heartwarming discovery to those who thought they already knew Shropshire but had not ventured beyond the areas in the west which have received the most publicity.

At Waters Upton (which did not get its name from its position near the river but is said to have originally been Walter's Upton, and named after Walter Fitzjohn, an early lord of the manor) many of the new buildings are of a nice, discreet, dark red brick which fits in well with the local colouring. The present church is a newcomer, built in the last century, but a Benefaction Board from 1715 shows that a church has stood there for a long time.

The Tern goes through Attingham Park to join the Severn, and slightly to the west is Upton Magna, a mixture of black-and-white and brick cottages, and one of the few Shropshire places to make anything like a traditional village picture with church and cottages neatly gathered round a small, tree-shaded green. The church was extended last century, but still retains some Norman features, and has a monument to Walter Barker, who died in 1644, which deserves close attention for its detail work. I must confess that I remember best the memorial in the churchyard to George William Corbet of Sundorne Castle (died 1906), lord of the manor and for fifty years rector of the parish, with its gloomy epitaph, "He tried to do his duty", which always reminds me of those cryptic entries on school reports. The scene is so peaceful at Upton Magna that it is difficult to realize that down by the river Tern at Upton Forge there was an ironworks where William Hazledine made the links for Telford's Menai Bridge. They were sent by canal to Shrewsbury to be tested. This was typical of the care that the engineer took to ensure that his structures would be safe. As an innovator he was treading on new ground and he did all he could to lessen the risks. The profession of civil engineering was born with his activities and it would profit present-day workers if they trusted less to theory and spent a little more time on similar practical tests.

When I first knew Shrewsbury, which was around 1930, it was a medieval town, but over the years and especially the last twenty it has been so altered that it has lost much of its old attraction. Yet, viewed from a distance where only the general outline of the town and the shape of the spires can be seen, it remains as inviting as ever; and although it is spreading, there are still places very near to it which are untouched. At Uffington, for instance, which is just across the river from the town and where there are a number of new bungalows, it is still possible to walk down a track by the church to the river bank and find a scene that might be miles from a town and many years from today.

The last part of this chapter covers the villages westwards around Wellington and out towards Wolverhampton. In such an industrial atmosphere they cannot be expected to have the remoteness and peace of those in the more rural areas, but some of them are worthy of mention and they are valued by people living over the border in Staffordshire.

The Shrewsbury branch of the Shropshire Union Canal made its way westwards through Withington, which now seems lost without its activity as if it were stranded on the shore. No doubt in time it will recover for it has the makings of a pleasant little group of buildings including the farm over the bridge by the church. At Longdon upon Tern there is a fascinating relic of Telford's early work. In 1795 he was busy with plans for the Ellesmere Canal and one of the major problems was the crossing of the Dee. At that time the standard method was to build a masonry bridge with puddled clay to hold the water, but at the Dee crossing this would have entailed a series of locks to get down to the river level and another chain to rise again on the other side, which would have slowed the traffic. Telford therefore suggested building out an embankment to lessen the gap and then constructing a high-level bridge, 1,000 feet long and 127 feet above the river, in which the canal would be carried in an iron trough. At that time he was also in charge of the building of the Shrewsbury branch of the Shropshire Union Canal and he saw an excellent opportunity to try this idea at Longdon upon Tern. The bridge still stands and is a striking example of an experimental undertaking which was itself useful over the years.

In this part of the county, from October to December, lorries with loads of sugar beet converge at the factory at Allscott which for this brief season bursts into a day and night activity to extract the sugar from the crop. The huge white plumes of smoke and steam rise high into the sky and make a dramatic sight by day; a lady I met there on one occasion told me that at night when it was lit up it looked like Blackpool illuminations, but I don't think the Lancashire resort would appreciate the comparison.

Wrockwardine and High Ercall which are nearer to Wellington are changing rapidly, but even in such places interest can be found by the watchful eye. At Bratton Road for instance, there is a most surprising bungalow which has the dazzling appearance of Jacob's coat, an effect obtained by its covering of cement slabs in which pieces of broken china have been set to form patterns. The bungalow was originally a hut which had been in use as part of the Agnes Hunt Hospital and the transformation had been the hobby of a tenant fifty years ago, Jesse Parker. By a strange chance the occupier in 1973 had as a girl taken broken crockery along to Mr. Parker while he was making the decorations.

East of the A442 going from Wellington to Whitchurch is Eyton upon the Weald Moors, another red brick place with a delightful end-of-the-road air about it. Even the eighteenth-century church is of red brick and fits into the pattern of the village. It has a fine, colourful window which Pevsner calls blatant, but then he did not have to live there before the roads were made up, when a lively splash of colour was very welcome to brighten a drab life, when the 'wild moors' were undrained and boggy.

Preston upon the Weald Moors sounds like a twin of Eyton and indeed it has the same red brick houses and also a red brick eighteenth-century church; but in addition it has a grand eighteenth-century hospital founded under the will of Lady Catherine Herbert as a thanksgiving for being rescued by the St. Bernard dogs when she was lost in the Alps. This a much more ambitious building than the usual modest almshouses and is like a great hall, with two-storeyed buildings lining three sides of a quadrangle.

After the open country of the Weald Moors, Kinnersley comes as a pleasant refuge with its great trees casting shade and all too often their leaves! The church has a most unusual outline, for when the tower was added in the seventeenth century the double bellcote was retained. When I visited the village in 1973 I found that air of uncertainty about it which a place gets just before it is developed and in the next few years it may be greatly changed.

Out on the far east of the county there is at this point a group of villages round Newport which is so far away from 'my' part of Shropshire and so near the border that I confess that I have always thought of them as belonging to Staffordshire. Heading in this direction there is, as a landmark, a monument at Lilleshall which stands so boldly on a hill that it seems that it must dominate the village. At closer quarters it becomes apparent that the village climbs so steeply up the far side of the hill that it reaches almost to the summit and the monument is on a small hillock at the end of a cricket field. But even close to, the obelisk is impressive for it stands seventy feet high; it was erected in 1839 to commemorate George Granville Leveson Gower, First Duke of Sutherland as a "public testimony that he went down to his grave with the blessings of tenants on his head". The view from the hill stretches far across Shropshire to distant peaks which are said to include the Clee Hills, the Wrekin, Haughmond Hill and 'occasionally' Plynlimmon.

The awkward setting of the village, poured over the top of a hill, prevents any very good groupings, but the church has a good position near the top. This is one of the oldest foundations in Shropshire, for there is said to have been a Saxon church on 'Lilla's Hill' in 670 and it was certainly well established at the time the Domesday survey was made. The present church dates from the early thirteenth century, although alterations have been made over the centuries. Recently it has been given a new character for the pews have been painted pale grey and the beams of the roof blue and red; colour is also evident in the recently restored arms of Charles I, a reminder of the loyalty of the Dukes of Sutherland to the Crown during the Commonwealth. The Levesons were connected with the village for four hundred years and among the monuments is an unusual one to Sir Richard (died 1661) and Lady Katherine (died 1674) Leveson which portrays them reclining on slabs in bunk fashion, with Sir Richard on the upper one.

Lilleshall is now well known for the training centre of the Central Council for Physical Recreation, which is housed in the old Hall of the Duke and some surrounding brick buildings. As the village is right on the boundary of Telford New Town great changes can be expected in the future. Below are the remains of Lilleshall Abbey. After the Dissolution the property was purchased by the Levesons, but it suffered badly in the Civil War when the Parliamentarians attacked it. Many of the stones were taken to build the nearby Lilleshall Grange and others were used in making the foundations for bridges on the canal.

Edgmond is now almost an extension of Newport with many new houses and there is little of the old village left, except the church, which has a grand tower and a gallery of gargoyles. Sundials are a particular interest of mine and I noticed that the dial in the churchyard bears the date 1753 and has a new motto for my collection, "As a shadow so is life". An unusual record in the church is that Pigotts were rectors from 1699 to 1888.

Chetwynd and Woodcote are little groups near the gates of the big estates of local landowners. Sheriff Hales is far more famous than its size would suggest, for the manor house was an academy for some of those who, in the seventeenth century, were barred by the Test Acts from Universities. Among those who attended was Robert Harley, later Lord Oxford. In more recent years it was the home of the late Mr. W. H. Slater's Ayrshire herd which kept the breed flag flying in the county at the time when the Friesians were becoming more and more popular.

Many places treasure a legend that a king or a queen slept within their walls, but few so dramatically as Boscobel to which Charles II fled after his defeat at Worcester in 1651. Despite popular belief this was not on Oak Apple Day, 29th May, but on 6th and 7th September. He hid in the crown of an oak tree during the day time and took advantage of a hiding place in the house at night. Unfortunately the tree in which he hid has now gone and visitors are shown one said to have grown from an acorn of the old tree.

Shifnal might have passed as a village some years ago, but after being whirled round it in the traffic on my last visit I have decided that now it must be a town.

After these disappointments, it was a pleasure to revisit Tong and find that it had improved since I last saw it. For years the traffic used to wind up past the church and there was no peace in the village. Now, however, a by-pass takes the vehicles to the other side of the church and the village street is quiet. Tong should add to its list of saints the name of the planner who was responsible for making the arrangements.

The great tower and spire of the church stand out as the village is approached and demand attention. However, inside, the church is so full of monuments that it is these which dominate it. There is a remarkable collection from Sir Fulke and Lady Elizabeth de Pembruge, the founder, to the many Vernons. In view of the prominence of this family in the church it is a surprise to discover that Tong passed from them to the Stanleys by marriage as long ago as the sixteenth century when Margaret Vernon married Sir Thomas Stanley, and that their son sold the estate in 1625, since when it has been owned by several other families. The old mansion of the Vernons was rebuilt in 1765 by Lancelot 'Capability' Brown for George Durant, and this in turn was demolished in 1954. The monuments therefore reflect a short period some hundreds of years ago. Yet such was the influence of the Vernons, that in the porch there is still a notice giving details of the occasions on which the Great Bell shall be rung, which includes whenever a member of the Royal Family visits Tong and when the head of the house of Vernon visits it.

Continuing southwards between Telford New Town and Wolverhampton there is a small chain of villages which are rapidly becoming urbanized. Albrighton and Donington are so close to Wolverhampton that they will soon be engulfed. Boningale hiding down a lane delighted one old lady I met who had moved there from the town and thought that it was perfect countryside, but after travelling round so many lovely villages it seemed but a shadow with its view across country scarred by a line of pylons. Beckbury has some nice cottages, but again is taking on the air of a suburb. In the church there is a reminder of earlier days in the incised slab of Roger Haughton, who died in 1505, and his wife. At its foot are ten neatly dressed children.

And so through Kemberton and Ryton, which latter greeted me with bells when I last went there—the ringers could be watched through a glass window in the tower. The village has so far managed to retain its peace and from the churchyard there is a secret view dropping steeply down to a valley.

And lastly Sutton Maddock, scattered along the main Wellington/Bridgnorth road, with the church and the Hall making a pleasant retreat over to the west. It will be many a day before I forget the sight of that grand tower standing boldly in the evening sun. It stood for all the spirit that has kept our villages inviolate over the centuries, and which will enable them to digest the influx of new building and rise again with a new attraction.

5

Around the Clee Hills

THE coloured contour map of Shropshire shows in the south-east a large triangular patch composed of Brown Clee Hill (1,772 feet) and Titterstone Clee Hill (1,750 feet) with low-lying land round the base like the moat of a sand castle. This makes a convenient section of the county to cover next; but although it is a tidy geographical division the villages vary as much as those in other parts of the county.

The north-westerly margin is marked by Corvedale and it was to Westhope above this valley that we moved for our second home in Shropshire. We looked out at Callow Hill which, with its square tower, became as familiar a landmark as the Wrekin had been at Acton Pigot, although it could not be seen from such distances. The tower, Flounders Folly, was built in 1838 by a Mr. Flounders to mark the point where four estates met.

Westhope cannot claim to be a village even by Shropshire's small standards for it is a mere hamlet lying up Seifton Batch, a narrow, slit-like valley at the south-west end of Wenlock Edge; but it has a village hall where popular whist drives and dances were held, and this earned it a certain amount of notoriety because people who had travelled up the seemingly unending narrow lane on dark nights used to swear that they had heard the wolves howling in the hills above. In true Salopian fashion the farmers of the valley added their own quota to the Westhope legend and claimed that their sheep could always be picked out in the market because their legs were longer on one side than the other as a result of living on the steeply sloping fields all their lives.

The main disadvantage was that it was in a very narrow valley, 600 feet up, so that the hours of sun were restricted and the growing season was short; indeed the farmers used to say that they had to wait till the snow was on their corn before it was ready to harvest. The difference was not very noticeable in mid-season, but in Spring the hedgerows down in Corvedale greened up a week or ten days before they did at Westhope.

Most of our shopping was done in Ludlow, about seven miles south along the B4365 road, a pleasant run especially in Spring when one stretch had its verge carpeted with white violets. The Corve here, for its last few miles before joining the Teme, is still quite small, but runs through a flat valley almost a mile across.

Culmington is the first village along the road. The school and inn are on the main road, but most of the village lies back along a rectangle formed by three minor lanes. It is one of those places which are always neat and tidy, and where there is never any sign of activity—even cleaning up. The church for years was noted in guide-books for its unfinished broach spire topped by a small lead spire. A manuscript in the British Museum has a painting dated 1793 showing the broach spire completed, but this must have been artist's licence because churchwardens' accounts of the time record payments for shingles and tiles for the small spire and its eventual covering with lead. By 1969 this had become crystalline and there was talk of replacing it with a plastic spire, but fortunately this horror was avoided and the church was given instead a top composed of six great aluminium vanes which meet to support a ball, making a very imaginative feature for an old church.

Culmington with Diddlebury was included in the lands of Corfham Castle on the other side of the river which was held by Walter Clifford, whose daughter Jane was Henry II's mistress, 'The Fair Rosamond'; Rosamond's Well is still marked near the scant remains of the castle.

Stanton Lacy, the next village towards Ludlow, lies just across the river and is one of those places which look like water-colour paintings come to life, with lush trees and a little lane leading up past the church to a T-junction where the rest of the cottages and farms lie. Although the village is named after the Norman de Lacy, the church has evidence of Saxon work which indicates that it existed before the Conquest.

Our way into Ludlow continued across the golf course which doubles as a race course—the road having to be closed for the few minutes of each race to allow the horses to cross. To the right here is Bromfield which has been changed so dramatically by the efforts of the road-makers that it is still difficult to recognize it. The village used to be a cosy little squiggle between buildings and over a picturesque bridge. Now the traffic is guided away over a bypass and, strangely, the village seems to have lost its atmosphere. No doubt eventually it will settle down again, for it has seen many changes in the past. At one time it had a twelfth-century Benedictine Priory, the half-timbered gatehouse of which still stands. After the Dissolution the chancel was used as part of a private house which was later burnt down. In 1658 the building reverted from domestic to religious use—a reversal of the present policy of the Church. It is thus a mixture of relics of the early Priory and seventeenth-century rebuilding. It has a wonderful painted roof which is a glorious concoction of clouds, angels and ribbons with texts, which succeeds because it is so exuberant; an illustration of the fact that if you are going to do something you should do it wholeheartedly.

A tablet in the church recalls the forgotten medical pioneer of Bromfield, Henry Hickman, who lived from 1800 to 1830. Surgery at that time was so painful that little progress was possible. Humphry Davy suggested in 1800 that nitrous oxide might be used as an anaesthetic but little was done to follow this up. Hickman began his own investigations to find some means of deadening pain during operations and, working while he was running his practice, by 1824 he had found that this was possible by using carbon dioxide. He reported his discoveries to the Royal Society and to the French Academy of Medicine but they were ignored and he died disappointed in 1830. Later when James Young Simpson discovered the use of chloroform, Hickman's work was mentioned but it was again ignored; and it was not until Henry Wellcome was forming his Historical Medical Museum that Hickman was eventually publicly acknowledged. The tablet in the church was put up in 1930 on the centenary of his death.

Turning to the left at the foot of Seifton Batch from Westhope, leads you along the B4368 road through the length of Corvedale. The road marks a sharp change in the countryside; to the north, narrow lanes climb up into the country of Wenlock Edge where there are small hamlets and isolated farms; while to the south in Corvedale there is rich, park-like countryside with lush trees.

The first village to be reached is Diddlebury, one of those place names with a deceptive pronounciation, for locally it is known as Delbury. There is, however, some justification in this case for the name of the old hall is spelt that way. Although the village now spreads out along the main road, its hub is still where the side road turns sharply uphill by a farm, with the square tower of the church standing boldly on the right and a pleasant line of cottages on the left. At the top of the hill is the school where we used to have to go to register our votes; a good excuse for a longer walk than usual! To some people the church may appear to be merely a rather dark building, but having visited many churches where a fragment of herring-bone masonry is regarded with reverence, it was a great delight for me the first time I went inside and found that the whole of the north wall is Saxon work. It looks so solid and formidable that it is difficult to credit that it is so old; it is equally remarkable that it has escaped being interfered with! For this wall alone Diddlebury is memorable.

Farms and cottages straggle along the B4368 so that it is difficult to place exactly the boundaries between such villages as Diddlebury, Aston Munslow and Munslow, although each has a well-defined centre. Aston Munslow's name is derived from the Saxon Estune or East Town. It is only an incident on a bend in the road, but up the narrow lane at the side of the 'Swan Inn' lies the White House which is acquiring fame owing to the devoted efforts of Constance Purser, the daughter of Mr. T. W. Purser who bought it in 1947. The earliest part of the building is a cruck hall

F

with spere truss in perfect condition dating from the fourteenth century. Alterations from that time onwards over the centuries can be traced; the greatest innovation was in 1780 when a Georgian wing was added after a fire. Now, aided by a band of helpers, Miss Purser is revealing the original building as far as possible. The Stedmans, who previously owned the house, are the family of Fabian Stedman who invented change ringing of bells. Although the sound of the bells across the meadow is pleasant on occasions, we have come to appreciate it rather less now that eager bands of bellringers tour the countryside descending on churches and ringing away for what seems like hours on end. Fabian has a lot to answer for.

Munslow proper is a little over a mile further along the road. It is a deceptive place, for most people see only the S-bend on the main road. This is charming enough, but the real village lies behind with the old church in a hollow and a cluster of modern houses discreetly tucked away out of sight. This is a gem of Corvedale, with a richness that is not usually found in Shropshire. The church standing with its sturdy tower and grand wooden porch in the leafy churchyard makes a perfect picture. Unfortunately it has been rather too eagerly restored in the past for the interior to match the promise of the first impression but it has some features that will satisfy those who go looking for curios—an incised tablet with an hour-glass and a skull; a brass to Richard Baldwin, which was restored in 1938 in memory of his kinsman, Stanley Baldwin, the Prime Minister with the pipe; and a brick from the Great Wall of China—a strange souvenir to bring round the world.

A weathervane might have been the best monument to Edward Littleton born in the village in 1589, for his opinions veered to suit the occasion. He at first supported the authority of Parliament against the Crown and then, on being made Solicitor General by Charles, he supported him in the Ship Money issue. Later he refused to seal the proclamation for the arrest of the five members and then sent the seal to Charles.

A few miles further on the road splits, the main arm going to Bridgnorth and the lesser one to Much Wenlock, passing first through Shipton, where it suddenly drops to present a fine view of Shipton Hall. It was built by Richard Lutwyche in 1587 and enlarged about 1750 when the imposing stable block, which looks grand enough to be a house, was added. Between these two buildings is a dovecot which has recently been re-roofed. Although Richard Lutwyche's son, John, rebuilt the chancel of the little church a couple of years after the hall was built, it does not match the magnificence of the residence and is modestly tucked away in the trees at its side. Most of the village lies hidden out of sight round the corner.

The road goes on to Much Wenlock over a series of ridges with a village in each dip. At Brockton a turning goes off towards the Edge and passes through Easthope, another place to make a picture, with the cottages posing beside the road and a neat little church which has been rebuilt since it was burnt out in the 1920s; the hour-glass used for timing sermons was salvaged and is one of the few to be seen in the county.

Bourton in the next dip spills down a road to the south with a large farm, a gathering of cottages, and a church with a weatherboarded belfry which can be seen through the trees. Bourton Manor, which was built at the end of the last century, incorporating parts of an earlier building, has a magnificent array of sixteen chimneys.

Much Wenlock was reduced in status in 1966, but still celebrated the quincentenary of its charter in 1968; so I will not venture to clash with tradition by suggesting that it might be a village.

The country on the other side of Corvedale lies on the slopes of Brown Clee Hill and resembles that on the side of Wenlock Edge, with winding lanes scrambling up and down between high hedges to find little tucked away villages. An inner circle of roads and villages lies parallel to the B4368 road about three miles west. The nearest to Ludlow of these is Stoke St. Milborough, named after Saint Milburga, King Penda's granddaughter, who founded the nunnery at Much Wenlock. Near the church a spring, known as St. Milburga's Well, surfaces where her horse's hoof struck the ground. The area has such a maze of brooks that it looks as if she had a very mettlesome nag which stamped around quite a bit!

Stoke has unfortunately deteriorated over the years and lost some of its quiet atmosphere, partly because of the erection of a number of sheds above the church. This church is a vast barn of a building which has always seemed empty to me; when I mentioned this to a neighbouring vicar he agreed that that was exactly the impression he had when he went there. One reason is that it is so tall, but another factor is that it is in a part of the county where there have always been small farms rather than large estates, so that there have not been people who could afford to give it much support or to fill it with memorials to their departed relatives.

Clee St. Margaret, a few miles north, on the other hand, is a cosy little place, even if its main street is always under water, for a brook runs for fifty yards along it in front of the houses, making it the longest ford in the county.

The road around Brown Clee becomes narrower and hillier but is delightfully tree-lined. Up the slope on the east is Nordy Bank, an Iron Age Fort which looms grimly in the evening light. A lane towards the Corve leads to Heath Chapel which stands like a deserted barn in a field by the roadside. When the key is turned the door is opened into yesterday. Within its whitewashed walls are a few box pews, a chancel arch, an old font and an air of peace. It is the simplest of Norman churches and it has a power that is never-failing. I was once there when a young lad and his girl came in; they stood and looked without saying a thing and then their hands sought each other. Eight hundred years of faith is magic. Below, nearer to the Corve, are Peaton and Bouldon. Bouldon is a charmingly homely place along the Clee Brook, only the painter's brush could do justice to it because the camera sees only the facts and the flaws, whereas the hand of the painter is guided by imagination and understanding.

Abdon seems to be perched high up till you notice that the open bellcote above the church has a wonderful backcloth of hillside rising up to Abdon Burf. It is an inspiring place in the sunshine, but must be remote when it snows. A mile and a half away down a steep hill, Tugford looks much more civilized. But Holdgate, although in gentler countryside, is like a deserted village. There are houses and farms, but I have never seen anyone, and the rather sad church looks equally deserted with signs of damp. It possesses one treasure, a Norman font which has well-preserved carvings of a dragon, interlace and foliage, round the bowl.

The influence of Corvedale is seen at Stanton Long only two miles away, which is a kinder, tree-filled place with pleasant houses, a farm with a great half-timbered barn, and a church which is approached by a downhill path through a tunnel of trees. This quick change of atmosphere is one of the delights of Shropshire for it means that even a short journey brings surprises and variety.

The roads coming northwards on either side of Brown Clee meet at Ditton Priors, which has the familiar pattern of a church and its churchyard in the middle of the village with houses and farms gathered round. Everything looks very peaceful now, but Ditton Priors has had conflicts and troubles in the past. For 125 years, owing to a dispute with the patron, the church had no vicar, and it was not until it was ruled in 1861 that a Catholic patron should not present to a Church of England parish that an incumbent was accepted. Industrially, too, the village has seen many changes. At one time this was a busy quarrying district and a railway ran down to Cleobury Mortimer. During and after the war there were Service establishments nearby, the last being American forces; but now these have gone and a hopeful notice points to "Ditton Priors Trading Estate".

Turning southwards to complete the circuit of Brown Clee, the first village you come to is Cleobury North which takes its name from the hill. It lies along a tree-lined stretch of the Bridgnorth/Ludlow road and looked much happier a few years ago, for now it bears the ugly scar of road improvements; perhaps time will improve things. When I was last there the church was being anxiously watched because there had been a theft from it. I found this fear in many Shropshire parishes and it would be a sad reflection on our age if it was remembered as the time when it became necessary to end the centuries-old tradition of the ever-open church.

A mile or so away Neenton perches above the Rea Brook; this was at one time known as the Neen, and the old name is remembered in a number of villages along the valley.

Among these homely places, Burwarton stands out strikingly as an estate village. For almost a mile Burwarton Park runs along by the road and the village has a number of those substantial, stone, establishment-type houses that are built by large estates. In the 1870s the church and the big house were rebuilt in local stone for the eighth Viscount Boyne by Salvin; the house has since been considerably altered. The influence of the family is even seen in the inn, the 'Boyne Arms', a fine Georgian building which has a resplendent sign with their arms. It has the unusual facility of a weighbridge outside.

The area between Brown Clee and Titterstone Clee is one of those backwaters that few people explore and it is made more remote because it is a tumult of hills with brooks running down the valleys between them. I spent many days following motorcycle trials through this area in the years before restrictions made things difficult for the organizers, and although this entailed much exploring of the lanes in the district, the villages are so hidden away that at that time I missed some of them. Loughton and Wheat-hill, for instance, both struggle down lanes from the main road to form concentrations round small churches.

The 'Three Horseshoes Inn' at Wheathill, however, is quite well known as a result of the unique auctions held there. Unlike the usual livestock auctions, these are held in a field and on a Saturday. Cecil Pritchard, licensee of the 'Three Horseshoes' told me that they were started well before the last war by the late Mr. Leonard H. Davies (after various amalgamations they are now run by McCartney, Morris and Barker). They were held on Saturdays to cater for the many local smallholders who had regular jobs and were only free on that day, and the sales had the additional attraction that the stock could be taken 'on the hoof', and if satisfactory prices were not offered they could be walked back home again without incurring any expense for transport. Despite changing circumstances the sales are still popular and are held monthly for cattle and, from August, fortnightly for sheep. The big sale is now the horse day on the first Saturday in October and in 1973, 200 horses were sold. This is also a big occasion for the 'Three Horse-shoes' because it stays open all day! Leonard Davies started other sales at Hungerford in Corvedale and the Angel Bank, Clee Hill, and in each case the site was within walking distance of an inn, which some suggest may have helped towards their success.

Even more hidden away are Silvington with a little Norman church; Farlow which is split, with part round the church and part round the old smithy; and Aston Botterell, a place that knew the Botterells for centuries, as is shown by the memorials in the church, which include an imposing monument to John Botterell who died in 1588 with his wife, and an incised stone slab to a fifteenth-century John and his wife. Their old manor house is now a farm-house which retains some of the earlier features.

To the north of the Clee Hill area there is a ring of villages centred on Bridgnorth. Monkhopton makes a welcome break along the B4368 road. It has a pleasant, tree-shaded corner with a well-kept farm, a colour-washed church with a slim tower, and Monk Hopton House which has a delightful garden open to the public under the National Gardens Scheme. Full effect has been obtained from a small rill that tumbles down the hillside by building water-falls and pools on the slope.

On a bend just before the main A458 road is Aston Eyre, with the church set on a rise on one side of the road and on the other a farmhouse which is on the site of the thirteenth-century manor house of the Fitz-Aers from whom the village takes its name. The little Norman church looks unpretentious but the tympanum showing Christ's entry into Jerusalem is judged to be one of the best examples of Norman work in Shropshire. It is intriguing to see how the artist appreciated the need to fill the space with the figures and even stretched the ass to accomplish this. The church itself is in need of care—let us hope that it does not get treated so much that it loses its original simplicity.

Part of the attraction of these two counties is the way that, off the main roads, life goes on in a way that ignores time. Tractors may have replaced horses and the unsightly television aerial spoilt the roof of an old cottage, but the mood is little changed. There is a good example of this at Acton Round which is only a little over a mile from the busy Shrewsbury/Bridgnorth road, but which stands at peace on a hilltop. There is a little group of cottages and a farm which has a modern folly in the shape of castellations added to a barn in a quite convincing way.

Lord Acton now lives in Africa but the family has ensured that the village will not be forgotten. It has the grand brick manor house built in the eighteenth century as a dower house; and in the church there is a monument with half-length figures of Sir Richard Acton (died 1703) and his wife holding hands. A little eighteenth-century chapel is dominated by an immense classical style monument to Sir Whitmore Acton (died 1731) and his wife, which has a dark sarcophagus between columns with an archway above. This is showing signs of crumbling and damp, as if it were mourning the departure of the family.

At Morville, in the church which stands by Morville Hall, an Elizabethan house rebuilt in the eighteenth century, there are many memorials to members of this family who lived at Aldenham Park a mile up the road towards Shrewsbury, showing how important they were in the area. Some had wider fame, especially Lord John Acton, born in 1834, who was a famous historian and politician and a close friend of Gladstone. The nave of the church belongs to the building consecrated in 1118 and much of the rest is also from Norman days. The church is blessed with a bell which has one of the most delightful tones I have heard in my wanderings. Perhaps it was their feeling for bells that led the local people to adopt the custom of ringing out a series of chimes to 'ring home' the deceased at a funeral instead of the more traditional tolling of a single bell.

Morville was probably the last place in Shropshire where the stocks were used. There is an amusing account by the police officer responsible for this. At the time, in April 1859, having failed to obtain a fine from a drunkard, he had him committed to the stocks which stood midway between the 'Acton Arms' and the turnpike gate. The officer discovered that for his part he had to stand 'watch and ward' over his prisoner during the six hours he was in the stocks and he feelingly described the duty as being worse than the punishment inflicted on the drunkard.

I have followed the Wheatland Hunt in the lanes near Tasley, which is rather appropriate because in 1831 the old Bridgnorth steeplechase course was laid out nearby

Astley Abbots, which lays back off the Broseley road, now looks like a residential suburb of Bridgnorth, though an old-established one; but it has a long history for the church was founded in 1138 and the chancel rebuilt in 1633. It has one of the best maidens garlands I have seen; faded copperplate writing records that it was hung in the church in remembrance of Hannah Phillips who died on 10th May 1707 on the eve of her wedding.

For over fifty years Albynes, a mile or so from Astley Abbots, was the home of the late Miss Frances Pitt whom lovers of the countryside will remember for her many books and articles filled with delightful stories and pictures of nature subjects. She was one of the pioneers; the nature photographers of today have equipment that makes their work easier and they have the example and experience of those like Miss Pitt and Oliver Pike to guide them. Some nature writers are one-sided people with a protectionist approach to their subject, but Miss Pitt had the rounded view of a true countrywoman. She was born at Oldbury Grange near Bridgnorth and when she was four years old the family moved to Westwood, a 200-acre farm. From that time until 1958 when she was 70 she was connected with farming and this gave her work the realistic approach that made it so refreshing. Over the years she kept practically every kind of British wild animal and wrote with great understanding of them, yet she was also for twenty-three seasons the Master or Joint Master of the Wheatland Hunt.

Linley and Willey are now two quiet villages, but they were once busy with the activities of John Wilkinson, one of the

Shropshire iron giants. Born in 1728 in Cumberland, the son of a labourer, by hard work and an almost fanatical belief in the possibilities of iron, he built up a large and prosperous business and pioneered many advances. He helped James Watt to make his steam engines a practical proposition by providing the accurately bored cylinders which were necessary; and the same boring machines enabled him to produce excellent pipes and cannon from which he made a fortune. In 1776 he installed one of Watt's engines to blow the furnaces at Willey; in 1787 he launched the first iron barge on the Severn; and in order to demonstrate that anything could be made of iron he even made iron coffins. For a spell the area throbbed with activity. The little Norman church at Linley has seen the changes come—and go. At Willey, a tree-lined road leads to a group of cottages standing near a pond, beyond which can be seen two ranges of stone stables, all that remains of Willey Old Hall which, in the nineteenth century, was replaced by the present hall which is some distance away in the park.

Across the other side of Willey Park is Barrow with fine views of the Wrekin and Wenlock Edge. It is a simple collection of houses, most of which are built of brick, including the almshouses which were founded in the seventeenth century and rebuilt on their present site in 1816. Although Barrow does not appear in the Domesday record, a church is believed to have existed since the ninth century and Saxon work in the chancel supports this idea. Even in this quiet spot there are reminders of the past industrial activity in the cast-iron monuments in the churchyard.

Other villages have not been so fortunate. Stockton on the Wellington/Bridgnorth road is much changed; and Badger was in a state of transition when I last visited it. Old buildings were being over-smartened up; thatched cottages were being re-thatched; an old farm building had a threshing-drum in it, while across the way new houses were being erected. It is difficult to imagine what future visitors will see; I can only hope that it will be in accord with the plaque on the front of a little row of cottages: "A.D. 1500. These cottages were reconstructed A.D. 1963 by Margaret Ruth in memory of her parents the Rev. Archibald William and Mrs. Mary Ethel Dicks who gave 50 years devoted service to Badger. We can only repay the debt we owe to the past by making the future indebted to us." This would be a good maxim to engrave on the walls of all Planning Departments.

Badger has already had other changes. The hall has been demolished and the church was restored in the nineteenth century, and even the font is a copy of that in St. Bride's church in Fleet Street. Among the monuments are some by well-known sculptors, including one by Chantrey of Isaac Hawkins Browne, who died in 1818 and is remembered as a good lawyer but a poor poet.

Another village which proved to me that in these days when changes can happen so quickly I could not rely on my memories of early visits, was Worfield. But there are signs of hope, for down by the church many of the old buildings have been modernized kindly and there is a block of flats and some old people's bungalows erected by Bridgnorth Rural District Council which show that with a little care it is possible to make additions to villages which fit in as well as the buildings which were erected by earlier generations. Of course, Worfield has a delightful situation in a bowl by the River Worfe and has been featured on the *Colourful Britain Calendar*, which no doubt encouraged the Council to have special regard for it, but it stands as an example which others might follow. The church with its tower and steeple rising to nearly 200 feet looks as if it had been waiting for the village to grow up, but in fact it has always been one of the largest parishes in England. Although it dates from the thirteenth or fourteenth century the church was so thoroughly restored that it has lost much of its old work. In the churchyard I found another unusual sundial for my collection, one showing the time in Worfield, Jerusalem and Mexico; it is difficult to think what use this information could have been to people in the village; perhaps it was simply a piece of gimmickry by the maker.

West of Bridgnorth and the Severn is an area which attracted the Normans and which is remarkable for the way in which families have remained on their estates for many centuries. At Gatacre Hall, Claverley, there are Gatacres claiming to have been there since the time of Edward the Confessor, and at Dudmaston Hall, Quatt, the Wolryche-Whitmore family have been in possession since the sixteenth century.

Claverley has a lovely grouping of buildings overlooked by another of the red sandstone churches which are a feature of eastern Shropshire. This is especially notable for the wall paintings discovered beneath many layers of colour wash in 1902: a strip about fifty feet long, in a style similar to the Bayeaux Tapestry, which is believed to show a battle between the Virtues and the Vices and to have been painted about 1200. Memorials honour generations of Gatacres: a fifteenth-century William Gatacre; General Gatacre who fought at Khartoum—the men called him General Backacher; and Captain Gatacre who died in World War I. There is also a striking memorial to Sir Robert Brooke, who died in 1558, and his two wives, one of whom was a Gatacre. Sir Robert who was Speaker of the House of Commons and Recorder of London, built Madeley Court now in Telford, and also lived for a time at Ludstone Court, a fine, stone-built house. This was restored in the 1830s in accordance with the original design and still has its moat filled with water and a beautifully kept knot garden in the grounds.

Hugo de Dudmaston was given Dudmaston in 1170 by Richard Strongbow. The site of his house is not known, but there has been a house in the present position since the sixteenth century. From the main road the drive goes across flat parkland to the house, and then the ground falls away sharply on the far side, so that from the terrace in front of the library there is a surprising view of a lake below. In the church at Quatt many memorials to the Wolryche-Whitmores trace the history of the family. Opposite is the eighteenth-century dower house, a massive well-kept building.

Quatford's church stands on a sandstone cliff overlooking the road and the Severn. It is said to have been built by Roger de Montgomery to fulfil a vow made by his wife, Countess Adelisa, during a storm, that if she reached shore safely she would have a church built at the spot where she met her husband. The dramatic nature of this stretch of the Severn valley has attracted other builders: there is a folly tower above the church, and on another cliff site a little nearer to Bridgnorth there is Quatford Castle with "fortifications and battlements" built in 1830.

Alveley has now been so changed by recent building development that it seems impossible that only a few years ago it was a small village centred around the church, but I remember visiting it to take pictures of some of the new bungalows for estate agents. This change was partly due to the opening of a shaft of the National Coal Board colliery in connection with the mine at Highley over the river, to which the coal was transported on an overhead wire line for dispatch by rail. About a mile north of the village is an old round-headed butter cross, which was probably used as a market during times of Plague.

The Severn is a barrier to east and west movement in this part of Shropshire for there is no bridge over it between Bridgnorth and Bewdley. This helps to keep the south of the county unspoilt, because both commercial and pleasure traffic tends to be 'streamed' by the bridges; but the lack of crossings causes problems for the local people and there have always been a number of ferries. Two of the most interesting are those at Hampton Loade and Arley, which is just over the border into Worcestershire. These both use the current as motive power. The ferry boat is attached by a running line to an overhead wire across the river, so that by throwing the long rudder in the required direction the ferry is swung sideways across the river; the return trip is made by reversing the position of the rudder. This simple device works quite well except when the line breaks, for then the boat is at the mercy of the river, and the Severn in full flood is merciless— when the Hampton Loade ferry was swept away in December 1964 the ferryman was drowned. For a time there was a doubt about its replacement, but a new ferry was launched in May 1965.

Hampton Loade is also the terminus of the Severn Valley Railway, one the lines run by groups of enthusiasts who enjoy driving real steam engines. This line operates a regular service along the four-and-a-half-mile stretch from Bridgnorth between March and October, thus allowing people to sample the pleasure of that delightful line which I used in the 1930s to avoid the hills from Shrewsbury to Worcester when I was taking a young lady on a cycling tour to the Vale of Evesham.

The country south of Bridgnorth between the Severn and Brown Clee is protected by the lack of river crossings and it is made more remote by the fact that it is very hilly with narrow roads and lanes. The road to Glazeley is typically adventurous, running through well-wooded countryside. The village is on a rising slope with a church rebuilt in Victorian days. The floor of the chancel is given an interesting appearance by a covering of soft green carpet. Unfortunately, this has been spoilt because a square has been cut out to enable the brass of Thomas Wylde, who died in 1599, to be seen. It does seem a shame to spoil the very fine effect in this way; if the brass experts had to be considered, the monument could have been taken up and fixed to the wall as has been done elsewhere.

Chetton is hidden away at the end of a road which climbs up an outlying spur of Brown Clee. It is said that Lady Godiva founded a church at Chetton, but if so it has vanished, for only the chancel of the present church is old and this is thirteenth-century work. The chancel arch rests on two large heads so economically cut that they are almost caricatures.

Middleton Scriven is one of those scattered villages which one is never sure one has reached till the far side is arrived at. Despite its isolation and small size, the church was rebuilt last century in that wholesale effort which cost us so many delightful churches. It was pleasant enough on an autumn day, but after living in the country for many years I always wonder what these far-away places are like in winter when the roads are snowbound.

There is a happier story at Upton Cressett than in many similarly remote villages. The grand Tudor brick hall had fallen into such a bad state that vandals were taking the panelling from the hall. Fortunately, new owners took it over just in time and aided by the Bridgnorth Rural District Council restored it in 1972. Such work is costly, but the result is more satisfying than a similar outlay on a modern property.

Sidbury owes its church to the same kind of privately inspired effort, for the building was burnt down in 1912 and the restoration was aided by Mrs. Clutterbuck who gave the stone for the work. Stottesdon, even deeper in the hills, has avoided such calamities and has some interesting Norman work in the church, including a very fine font covered with carvings which are probably from the Herefordshire school which did such fine work at Kilpeck and Eardisley.

After such explorations of the minor ways, it is a relief to come out on to the B4363 which seems like a main road. Unfortunately, this easier access has encouraged development at Eardington, Chelmarsh and Billingsley. I feel rather contrite about Billingsley where we used to gather at the 'Cape of Good Hope' Inn where there were motorcycle trials in the area, because I took some photographs to show the views from some of the early plots to be built on, so that in a way I helped the project.

After so many modest places, Kinlet suggests the prospect of something more imposing because Kinlet Knoll was part of the dowry of Edward the Confessor's wife, Edith, but the original village has disappeared and now there is little in the gathering of cottages at the entrance to the hall to indicate its long history. The red brick Kinlet Hall was built in the eighteenth century, so that also is a newcomer to the scene. Not surprisingly, it is in the church that the history is found, for this has some of the original Norman work, although there have been additions over the centuries. The monuments trace the owners of Kinlet. The earliest is Lady Lychfield of 1415; later are the Blounts, including Sir George Blount who died in 1584, whose memorial includes his wife, daughter and son, another of those unfortunate children reputed to have died while eating fruit—an apple in this case; the reredos is in memory of Captain Charles Childe who fell in South Africa; and a brass commemorates another member of that family killed at Vimy Ridge.

The value of the estate lay in the timber, and for centuries Kinlet oak was highly valued, especially for ship-building. It is fashionable to criticize the present times for wasting precious resources without thought for the future, but past generations were little wiser and our timber was used up with little thought as to future supplies and only a few 'cranks' raised the alarm.

Just north of Cleobury Mortimer in the valley of the Rea Brook is Neen Savage with a deep ford at the end of it. This situation was no doubt responsible for the growth of paper-making in earlier times, but there is no trace of industry now. There was a smell of smoke in the air when I last visited the village, for a builder who was doing some work had first to clear away the leaves and grass cuttings which had been thrown against the walls. It was a rather suitable scent, for in 1825 a fire broke out in the church and the screen was only saved by the action of Thomas Hall, in whose memory it was later restored.

Some Salopians may query the inclusion of Cleobury Mortimer, for it is almost a town by local standards; but it is administered by Ludlow Rural District Council and it has the comfortable feel of a village. Soaring above the other buildings is the crooked broach spire of the church, which is Cleobury's trade mark. The twist is said to be due to the warping of the shingles. In the porch is a strange fourteenth-century stoup with an Egyptian look about it. The east window of the church was inserted in 1875 as a memorial to William Langland, the author of *The Vision of Piers Ploughman*. This poem appeared about 1362 and is re-garded by scholars as being as important as Chaucer's work, but it lacks the popular appeal of the Canterbury Tales.

The Ludlow road climbs up out of Cleobury passing Hopton Wafers which lies back up a valley. New buildings are going up, but round its centre there are some pleasant old houses and a great beech tree gives the scene a restfulness. The church, which was rebuilt in 1827, has a remarkable monument to Thomas Botfield showing him pointing to Heaven, with his mourning wife beside him.

The road steepens as it climbs Clee Hill, a shoulder of Titterstone

A view in Hope Dale at the southern end of Wenlock Edge

The doorway at Kilpeck church

The brass to Dame
Margaret Chute at Marden

At work in the new Mortimer Forest

"Is my seam straight?"—a ploughing match

Emptying hops in the oasthouse for drying

Efficient handling speeds selling at Craven Arms

Clee Hill. Although at 1,750 feet this is twenty-two feet lower than Brown Clee Hill, it is usually regarded as the 'Big One' by most people, for it is so prominent on the skyline. It is also better known because the main road runs along it for some distance over the 1,000 feet mark before dropping down the infamous Angel Bank. It is said that from the road on the right day the Bristol Estuary can be seen, but I have never been able to confirm this.

The older settlement is at Doddington where there is a church built in 1849, but now the main village is Clee Hill about two miles further along and immediately before the descent. Situated at 1,243 feet above sea level, it is an untidy collection of houses which probably started as homes for the workers in the quarry which is eating into the hard stone. It seems one of the most inhospitable places in the county and Ludlow folk watch with a ghoulish pleasure as cloud and snow cover it; yet new houses are being built there.

On the steep slope on the Ludlow side of the hill is Bitterley, gathered in a casual fashion round a meeting of roads. The past importance of the village is indicated by the fact that the school was founded in 1712 by John Newborough, a former headmaster of Eton, as a grammar school, a status which has helped it to keep open when so many village schools are being closed. Standing apart from the village is Bitterley Court, the ancient home of the Walcots, and the church of which they have been patrons. It is a lofty building with monuments to the families of the Court and also of Henley Hall. Especially striking is a huge wall monument with an obelisk to Littleton Powys who died in 1731. The present family at Henley Hall has given the church a fine reredos and built the old screen upwards to include a loft. A monument which receives much attention is one showing a kneeling figure between two columns; this is Timothy Lucye who died in 1616 and who was a grandson of Sir Timothy Lucy who is supposed to have been the original Mr. Justice Shallow in Shakespeare's play, *The Merry Wives of Windsor*.

Middleton lies at the bottom of the hill, almost opposite Henley Hall, which was built for Thomas Powis in the seventeenth

G

century. It has been much altered over the years, especially in 1875 and 1907 after it had been purchased by Edmund Thomas Wedgwood Wood who had connections with the Wedgwood pottery family. The village wanders up a lane with no real cohesion but a nice sense of togetherness till Middleton Court House and the church are reached.

Between the high-climbing road over Clee Hill and the A456, which links Kidderminster and Ludlow, there is another of those areas with tiny villages tucked away in wooded valleys between hills. They are so difficult to reach that it is a surprise to find them, yet some have long histories. There is Neen Sollars, for instance, in the wandering valley of the Rea Brook. In a pleasant street wandering downhill past an inn, there is a cruciform church which looks very ambitious for such a place. A monument in the south transept reveals that at one time the manor was held by the Coningsbys, for it has the figure of Humphrey Conyngsby, who died in 1624, now looking rather out of place in his magnificence. He is remembered as "a perfect scholar by education and a great traveller by his own affection".

Milson nearby, is even smaller, with a church which has the defensive type of tower more usually seen in the Clun area; Coreley, scattered along little roads, has its church set up on a steep bank; Nash, Knowbury, Hope Bagot and Whitton are higher up the slopes of Clee Hill; while Boraston is perhaps the prettiest of the group with some nice old houses and a church that was greatly restored last century and has a font that came from Buildwas. Greete, despite its welcoming name, is no easier to get to, but being built mainly of brick has a warmth that tempers its position.

After the simplicity of these tiny places it is a change to discover Burford near to the Worcestershire border. The village does not lead one to expect the church and great house which are down a narrow lane, and which show how important the place was when the Cornwall family lived there. Since then it has had varied fortunes with high spots in the early eighteenth century when William Bowles bought the estate and built the new Burford house, and again when the Rushouts owned it. This family restored the church in 1889 and created its present atmosphere. The monuments tell the story of Burford's early greatness. There is an alabaster figure of John of Gaunt's daughter, Princess Elizabeth, who died in 1426; a painted wooden figure of Edmund Cornwall who died in 1508; and the strange triptych to a later Edmund who died in 1568. This is a huge wooden affair eleven feet high with doors that open to reveal full-size figures of Edmund with his father and mother, while a lower narrow panel shows him lying full length in his shroud—and full length was said to have been seven feet three inches. He is reputed to have been "very sweet of nature"; but a person of that size can afford to be sweet!

Nearer to Ludlow, Caynham is now being developed as a residential area, but it is an ancient settlement with an early British camp on the hill above it, and although the church was rebuilt in the last century it has some Norman parts, including an unusual triple arch.

The twin villages of Ashford Carbonel and Ashford Bowdler are on opposite sides of the River Teme south of Ludlow. Ashford Carbonel has a pleasant street with Ashford Court at the end. The church has a vesica window, an early Christian symbol. Ashford Bowdler is smaller and cut by the railway but has some pretty cottages.

Ludford, just across the river from Ludlow, is taken by many people to be part of that town, but it deserves to maintain its separate identity for it has some delightful homes, and the cottages beside the 'Old Bell' have particularly fine chimneys. The memorials in the church show that in the past Ludford had its own standing for there are memorials to the Foxes and to Sir Job Charlton, Speaker of the House of Commons, who might have been expected to have been buried in the larger church in Ludlow. And Ludford certainly has the last word for from Whitcliffe, near the 'Ludlow Arms Hotel', which has a brick wall thirty-five feet high for its fives court, there is the best view of Ludlow's famous castle.

6

The Clun Valley—
Sheep and Housman

WHEN the Clun Valley is mentioned, many people immediately think of Housman Country and fumble in their memories for the lines:

> Clunton and Clunbury,
> Clungunford and Clun,
> Are the quietest places
> Under the sun.

Although this is the opening of *The Shropshire Lad*, the lines are in fact a local rhyme which he borrowed and there are many less complimentary versions, such as:

> Clunton, Clunbury,
> Clungunford and Clun,
> The four drunkenest places
> Under the sun.

Housman is now firmly associated with the county but he was not a Salopian, for he was born at Fockbury, near Bromsgrove in Worcestershire, and lived in that county. And despite the fact that his descriptions of the countryside are often quoted, he himself confessed that he used some of the place names merely because they fitted his metre or scheme of rhymes. Still, the poems have drawn attention to the county in a way that no native verse would, for no true Salopian would write a poem about his county unless it had a sting in its tail.

It would be fairer if this area was called the Vale of Sheep, for the Clun Forest breed is known all over the country and nowadays there are a number of flocks overseas. The Clun Forest sheep are compact animals which can be easily recognized by their dark faces. They are valuable on the farm because they produce both high grade wool and excellent meat; and the ewes are good mothers, looking after their lambs well so that they are easy to manage.

The Clun Valley was for many years one of the routes along which farmers from Wales brought their stock to sell in England. The combination of the local interest in sheep and the influx of stock from Wales led to the growth of Craven Arms, situated where the B4368 road from the border crosses the A49 and goes on up Corvedale to Bridgnorth and the Midlands. Craven Arms is that rare phenomenon, a modern village. The exact date of its beginning is not known, but the 'Craven Arms', the inn from which the village takes its name, is first mentioned only at the beginning of the nineteenth century. The coming of the railway gave further importance to the village because it became a junction for the line through Central Wales.

Then in 1874 Rogers and Hamer held the first of the annual sheep sales which have made Craven Arms famous throughout the country. By 1899 there were two firms of auctioneers, Messrs. Jackson and McCartney and Messrs. Marshall and Poole, each of which had their own field for their sales, but these have now amalgamated.

Buyers have always come from all over the country to the sales and there are some old timers who talk of the days when sheep were walked to their new pastures in Leicestershire and other eastern counties. Later, the railway carried the sheep and as many as 320 trucks were loaded after the sales. A year that is still remembered is 1949, for on checking through the list of buyers, it was found that sheep had been sent to every county in England and Wales.

The sales are held during August and September and up to 20,000 sheep may be sold in a day. A field beside the railway is converted into a stockyard by erecting rows of iron hurdles to form pens. All is ordered chaos as the sheep are unloaded and driven to their pens, till by a miracle they have settled down by eleven o'clock when the ringing of a hand bell indicates that selling will commence. An important factor for buyers is the hardiness of the sheep reared on the hills, and as each lot is brought into the ring the auctioneer announces the situation of the farm, many of which are above the 1,000-feet contour. Ewes are usually sold in pens of forty and practised teams of drovers keep them moving in and out of the ring at lightning pace, but even with two rings and a team of auctioneers working in relays, selling goes on till 5.30 p.m.

Centuries before Craven Arms existed, Stokesay a mile south had its castle. This is strictly a fortified manor house originally built in 1240. It passed to Laurence de Ludlow who was granted a licence to crenellate, and added the south tower and the castellated wall. The north tower has a timbered upper storey which was added in the seventeenth century, giving the castle a curiously dual character: from the south it looks like a miniature fortress; while from the north it seems as if it has come from the pages of a fairy tale. The timber-framed gatehouse is another late addition, from the sixteenth century, and is a gloriously exuberant piece of work with many carvings. In 1645 the castle was besieged by Cromwell's troops and was later slighted, but it was lived in till 1727, after which it was used as farm buildings. The Allcroft family bought it in 1869 and since then they have cherished it so that now it is one of the most striking examples we have of a fortified manor house.

Beside the castle is the church which is equally worthy of a visit, although it is not as old as many of those in Shropshire, and the present building was erected about ten years after the original church had been practically destroyed, at the time of the siege of the castle. The high pulpit has to its side the canopied pew of the lord of the manor, and faces rows of box pews. With the gallery at the west end, the impression is of a wealth of woodwork. A modern touch in the church is a window to Lieutenant

Hotchkiss who was killed on 10th September 1912 in Oxford-shire and was the first Shropshire man to be killed in an air accident.

The River Onny, the A49 road and the railway, squeeze along the valley towards Ludlow and become entangled in complicated crossings reminiscent of old-time dancing at Onibury, where the railway crosses the river and then the road at a level crossing, after which the road crosses the river. The village tucks itself back off the road and is much more peaceful than appears likely. Up the lane at Walton is the home of Roy Jones who has followed his father into thatching and is finding a ready demand for his work over a wide area. There is a particularly fine roof done by him on the green at Brampton Bryan.

North of Craven Arms the valley of the Onny turns into the hills at the Grove, where there is a large chicken processing unit which is providing work for many people for miles around. The fact that the firm has to run its own bus to collect workers shows how poorly the area is served by public transport. Wistanstow is a stone-built village where the gardens are so full of flowers that it looks quite gay. It was sited for safety on a shoulder of the hill above the valley The church, dating from around 1200, points to the antiquity of the settlement which is believed to take its name from Saint Wystan, the heir to a ninth-century king of Mercia, who was killed by his uncle.

Edgton, deeper in the hills, is built on the side of a slope so steep that many of the houses look out on to their neighbour's roofs. The church is at the top, a little place where box pews and sombre slate memorial tablets help to retain the atmosphere despite the fact that it was largely rebuilt at the end of last century.

Hopesay, as its name suggests, is in a valley and this, with its many trees, gives it a homely atmosphere despite the fact that all around hills rise up to over 1,000 feet. The church stands above the village and has a great tower topped with a little pyramid turret. This is a style which is peculiar to this border area and was probably built as a refuge in the first instance. A strange feature of the church is that the nave is more decorative than the chancel, with a roof interestingly divided into panels and two mosaics in the wall giving a sparkling touch of colour. A little stream goes down to the Clun Valley which is the next area to cover.

Unlike many local villages, church and cottages were originally apart at Clungunford, so that it is mainly new properties which are around the church, a much restored building which seems too large for the village. It is also unusual in that most of the interest is in the newer things. The tower and porch with its carvings of St. Cuthbert were both part of the nineteenth-century rebuilding, and there is a window in memory of Margaret Ellen Vaughan of Abcott which shows a view of the local countryside with the church and includes a picture of a modern shepherd—an interesting change from the more usual ecclesiastical subjects.

Aston on Clun, about a mile north, has at its centre the very shorn remnant of the Brides or Arbor Tree, which stands as a warning to those who would like to keep old customs alive. Every year on 29th May the old tree had been decorated with flags provided in memory of Mary Carter of Sibdon Castle nearby, who had been delighted to see it beflagged on the occasion of her marriage to Robert Marston in 1786. This dressing of trees on 29th May is often associated with the Oak Apple Day celebrations of the restoration of King Charles in 1660, but in many cases it has an earlier origin, in the heathen fertility rites when Brigit was worshipped. Later she was sanctified as St. Brigit or St. Bride. At Aston on Clun it was the custom to give young brides a cutting from the tree and if this struck it was a token that they would be blessed with large families. The Marston family died out in 1951, so in 1954 the provision of flags was taken over by the parish council which had ambitions for wider fame. Member countries of the Commonwealth were invited to send their flags to put on the tree and by 1959 the ceremony had become such a nationally known event that when Princess Margaret was in the area she made a special detour to see the tree. Unfortunately the publicity focused attention on the heathen origins of the custom and led to objections, so that in 1960 there were no children to dance round the tree and no more cuttings for new brides. One of the first girls to have missed the heathen blessing on her marriage confessed to me that even after many years she still felt something was missing from her wedding. Despite this she had two daughters, so all was well. These events appear to have disheartened the old tree for it began to wither away until drastic surgery was needed. Now it is green again, although only a shadow of its former self. Maybe as it regrows it will be restored to favour in the village.

Aston is an individual sort of place in other ways. It has an oddly named 'Kangaroo Inn' and also two round houses. With hopes of seeing a family seated at a round table I went into one of these, but was disappointed to find that with a division down the centre, and suitably arranged furniture, it had been given the appearance of a normal-shaped room with a curved bay window.

At Little Brampton the way to Clunbury is indicated by an unusual signpost which has the place names cut out on metal arms. This is said to have been set up in 1800 by Lord Clive. Clunbury is perhaps the village in the rhyme most deserving of the tag of being quiet, for it is comfortably jumbled in the valley below Clunbury Hill, a place of timber and stone houses which is bright with flowers and has an appealing air of idleness.

Poor Clunton on the main road along the valley suffers from a constant stream of traffic which seems to have riven it apart, so that it cannot be called quiet any longer. The small chapel which was rebuilt in 1870 is more interesting than its outside, for steps up to the choir and altar give it a special atmosphere.

And finally to Clun, which is quite large compared with the other villages in the valley. It is one of several places in this part of the county which had charters as boroughs and have now lost that status. In the case of Clun this change was in 1886 and although the Clun Town Trust still has the silver maces of 1580 and 1614, the place now has the feel of a village for those visiting it. It stands on one of those natural defensive points which have been important throughout history. There are signs of ancient camps, including one attributed to Caractacus, and the castle, of which now only fragments remain. As so often happens this is best viewed from a distance, and from the Bishop's Castle road it can be seen standing out in the valley with the river to aid its defence. Sir Walter Scott was in Clun while gathering material for *The Betrothed*, and it is suggested that the castle was the original for the Garde Dolereuse, but the description in the book could fit many border strongholds.

Clun is strangely divided, the castle and other old buildings being on one hilltop with most of the shops; while the church is on the other hill across the river, at the top of a rather more impressive looking street. The church has the typical border tower with a little pyramid cap and some good woodwork inside.

Bishop's Castle had a mayor and council until 1967 and still retains the air of a town, so in deference to its ancient standing it will not be classed as a village. One part of the town's story must be included, and that is the railway which ran along the Plowden Valley from Craven Arms. It was hoped that this would bring great benefits to the area, but it proved to be a faltering link. The railway scheme was approved by Parliament in 1861 and on 24th October 1865 the first train arrived at Bishop's Castle. This proved to be merely a gesture, and a rather premature one, for the train was borrowed from another company and the station was not even built. The next passenger train ran on 1st February of the following year. The line ran through Plowden, Eaton and Lydham Heath, but the people of the area could not have been very railway minded because before the end of the first year's working the company was in financial difficulties and bailiffs were appointed to ride on all trains. Despite other difficulties such as a flood, sheep on the line and a landowner who removed part of the rails to secure payment of outstanding rent, the Bishop's Castle Railway continued into the 1930s when at last its track was dismantled.

Nearby are Lydham and More which always seem to go together like William and Mary, perhaps because I am so used to seeing their names together on signposts. Yet they are quite different. Lydham on the A489 Newtown road appears to be quite urban with only the little church retaining an air of age—and *it* was largely rebuilt in the nineteenth century. More on the other hand, is an attractive place with that familiar Shropshire pattern of farms and cottages set round the church. The raised churchyard fills the centre of the square with the buildings pressing close round it, almost giving the impression of one of those famous squares that used to be formed by English armies.

The Mores are one of those families that came over with William the Conqueror and, receiving land then, have held it ever since. During the Civil War they were one of the few ancient families of Shropshire to support the Parliamentarians and Samuel More was in command at Hopton Castle and was taken prisoner after it fell. He was later exchanged, and held important posts till he was suspected of plotting to depose Cromwell, which resulted in his exclusion from Parliament. His son Robert was a botanist with the dubious claim to fame of having planted the first larches in this country.

The church reflects the standing and the sobriety of the family, with a relatively large More Chapel that was built in 1640 and later enlarged, but which has only modest memorials to the family. There is a splendid coat of arms in brass on the floor and the only memorial with a figure is that to Harriott Mary More who died in 1851. Also in the chapel is a press of books presented with rules for their use by Richard More in 1680. Around the font is a portion of a Roman pavement found in the grounds of Linley Hall where the Mores have lived for centuries. Their old castle has gone, but the Hall, built in 1742, stands imposingly at the end of a long avenue.

Although this area is away in the hills there are several large estates. South of More is Walcot, the old home of the Walcots. This was purchased by Lord Clive who practically rebuilt it as a large, red brick house, and it later passed by marriage to the Earl of Powis who sold it this century. Plowden Hall is an Elizabethan, timber-framed house built by that family. Each of these old families has a transept in the church at Lydbury North. The chapel on the north belongs to the Plowden family, one of whom built it as a thanksgiving for his safe return from the Crusades; the Walcot Chapel on the south was built by the family on the restoration of King Charles II, and has an upper storey which was used as a school room at one time. The most imposing feature of the church is a great tower in which there is a single-handed clock.

The hills south of the Clun Valley rise up to nearly 1,500 feet and roads wind among them to little villages. One of the best is Hopton Castle which has quite prominent remains of its castle in a field by the road junction. This is a puzzling site to have built a castle for it does not look strong, yet the Keep dates from Norman times. Perhaps the brook was a better defence in earlier days. The castle's most famous engagement ended in defeat. This was during the Civil War when, with thirty-one men, Samuel More held out for three weeks against the Royalists; when at last they surrendered, all the men except More were shot. Now the village looks too peaceful even to engage in a snowball fight. Despite its position in the hills the village has some very fine trees, and there is a grand oak over by the Victorian church, which is built on a slope across the fields from the village. Perhaps this is why there are some good timber-framed barns to be seen?

A couple of miles south along a quiet little lane which has some fine views across the valley is Bedstone, a pleasant place with a little old church with a fine array of deep-set windows, which take up much of the walls of the nave. Bedstone Court, a Victorian black-and-white house, is now used as a school.

Bucknell, almost on the border with Herefordshire, deserves special mention because it has a railway station, a distinction which so few villages in this area possess that it is almost necessary to describe what it is! Fortunately this has not turned the village into a commercial metropolis. There are a few businesses near the station, but away from these there are some pleasant houses round the church, which has an unusual enamelled clock dial and was rather over-restored in the days when the big house beside it was the home of the family who owned the countryside around. Now the outbuildings and stables have been converted into very attractive flats which share the old stableyard. This is one of the most successful conversions of this type which I have seen and it has created a very happy community.

The railway line and road go along together to Knighton in Radnorshire round Stow Hill; and up a lane lies Stow, one more of those places which look like pictures out of Victorian sketch books, if the tractor in the farmyard is overlooked. The narrow road becomes a lane and after passing the farm rears up the side of a hill as a track which stops by a little group of cottages and a church. When I was in Colombo during the war I used to wonder what the local people made of the slick American comedies shown at the cinema. The scenes of life in our cities brought by television to such country areas as this must seem just as far away and fanciful. There is a tiny church with a weatherboarded belfry. Inside there is a surprise, for instead of the expected modest setting there is a fine roof with tie beams, queen posts and decorative panels. Colour is added by a reredos and panels in mosaic of stone, copper and mother-of-pearl.

The border with Wales runs along the Teme Valley here for many miles switching from side to side in a most unusual manner. Llanfair Waterdine is an outpost of the county with a fine old bridge and a church which lost most of its carving in a restoration during last century, but some portions still remain and have an inscription in Welsh, showing that the county border has crossed to the far side of Offa's Dyke.

This great earthwork runs from Prestatyn on the North Wales coast to Chepstow at the mouth of the Severn. In places the line can only be guessed at, but in this part of the country there is no doubt. High up on Llanfair Hill at over 1,300 feet the Dyke can be seen running for miles across the open countryside, a high bank with a ditch in front of it. A legend has it that the Dyke was made in a single night by the Devil himself driving a plough drawn by a gander and a turkey-cock. In fact like most things it was done by sheer hard work and it stands as a memorial to Offa, King of Mercia, who lived in the eighth century. This period of history is usually referred to as the Dark Ages and information is scant; indeed the account of the building of the Dyke comes from an early manuscript, *The Life of King Alfred* written by Asser, a Welshman.

Offa became King of Mercia in 758 and gradually extended his kingdom till his importance was such that Charlemagne suggested a marriage between his son and one of Offa's daughters; an arrangement which fell through because Offa insisted that in return his son should marry one of Charlemagne's daughters. There is a quite modern note in the fact that as a result of this dispute trading between England and the Continent was broken off until a new trade agreement was made in 796.

The Dyke was built between 784 and 796 as an agreed border with the Welsh in an attempt to bring peace to the area. It is a remarkable piece of work that entailed considerable organization of forces and it is as well surveyed as the work of the Romans, striking boldly across the open moors, taking advantage of natural formations and in places conceding points such as Chepstow and Tintern, which were apparently important at the time to the Welsh. The present-day border between the two countries still runs approximately on the line of the Dyke. In 1971 the Dyke stepped into the twentieth century when the Countryside Commission's Long Distance Footpath was opened along the same route.

From Llanfair Hill the Dyke crosses Spoad Hill and then drops down to Lower Spoad Farm, Newcastle. The old farmhouse has an Elizabethan oak overmantel beam with striking carvings in the style of Norman work. Newcastle itself seems mainly modern —even the church is only just over a hundred years old—yet earthworks on the hills around show that the site had prehistoric importance as the key to the valley.

The first few miles of the Dyke north of Lower Spoad Farm are not quite so striking as it follows a contour-hugging line through the hills, but at Mainstone and over Edenhope Hill it gets into its stride again and there are some magnificent stretches. Mainstone lies down in a valley and was once an important trading point. It takes its name from the large stone—*maen*—which is kept at the church. This may have been used as a weight, but its reputation is now as a trial of strength: strong men were said to lift it up and toss it over their shoulders. As it weighs two hundredweights this might seem a difficult and dangerous feat, but, until recently, farm workers used to carry sacks of wheat weighing two and quarter hundredweights as a regular task.

Above Mainstone is the lonely waste of Clun Forest, an expanse of moorland rising in places to over 1,500 feet. It is an inhospitable place and in the past it must have been even more so. One tragedy is marked by the Cantlin Stone and a nineteenth-century cross. On the stone can just be read the inscription "WC decsd here Buried 1691 at Betws". The WC was William Cantlin, a pedlar who collapsed and died at the spot in 1691. No relatives could be traced and the villages around did not want the trouble and expense of burying him, but eventually his body was taken to the churchyard at Betws y Crwyn. The incident might have been forgotten, but there was a strange sequel 184 years later in 1875 when the Clun Forest Enclosure Act was being passed. Then the fact that the village had assumed responsibility for the burial was accepted as proof of its authority over the area and it was granted a considerable extra tract of land. The incident so impressed Beriah Botfield, M.P. for Ludlow, that he set up the cross beside the stone. Betws is still only a scattered place in the hills, with a little church which has some fine woodwork, including a medieval screen and a fine array of pews which have the names of the local farms on them.

The road from Clun climbs up until, by the 'Anchor Inn' it looks out over the border to Radnorshire. This is the way that latter day Welshmen brought their livestock into market and there are still traces of the pounds they used along the road. The inn is said to have got its name from the fact that a sailor who had retired came along the road from the coast and was so delighted with the view that he dropped anchor and stayed there. Whether or not this is true it is a fitting place to end the section on Shropshire villages.

7

Into Herefordshire—
The Eastern Borderland

A COUNTY is much more than an area arbitrarily drawn on a map. Although the wandering lines of the boundaries may annoy neat-minded planners who would like everything to be straight and logical, they have a real significance and a long tradition behind them. The differences between counties can be seen in the buildings, the type of farming, the style of hedging and the people themselves. Under the new arrangements for local government, Herefordshire and Worcestershire have been amalgamated to make what is called a 'viable authority'. Apparently it has the right number of inhabitants, but only a computer could see the reason in creating such a vast area of nearly a million acres with a boundary 230 miles long. The workers in the factories of Kidderminster and Redditch, and the market gardeners of the Vale of Evesham can have little common interest with the farmers rearing beef cattle in Herefordshire. County loyalties, however, are based on deeper things than the position of the council offices. Herefordshire will remain apart in spirit, a haven where the sands of time run slowly.

When we moved to the county from Shropshire it seemed a richly green place which gave us the feeling that we had moved much further south than the map showed to be the fact, and the people matched the kindliness of the scene. I have lived in many parts of the country and did not expect ever to find another area

The gatehouse at Stokesay seen through the church lychgate

Topiary at Woonton

Topiary at Stoke Prior

'Border Fan' corn dolly at Eye Manor

Vats at Weston's cider works

Goodrich Castle seems to grow out of the rock

HEREFORDSHIRE

H

where the people were as friendly as those of Manchester, but the Herefordians made us welcome on the first day that we arrived and we have never felt we were aliens. Every other newcomer to the county that I have spoken to has been warmed in the same way by the friendliness with which they have been accepted, without that initial period of wariness which is so often encountered.

Nowadays people move about much more than they used to and many present-day Herefordians were not born in the county, so it seems that this characteristic is not inherited but comes from the contentment of living in such a green and pleasant countryside away from the pressures which create the stresses and bad tempers found in towns. Herefordshire is shaped like a giant bowl with a rim of hills around the borders which helps to keep off much of the bad weather, and within this rim is a central plain where there is so much sky that heaven seems very near. The city of Hereford has a population of 47,000; Leominster the second largest town has 7,500 people; there are only a few other towns and most of these would pass as villages in many counties. The villages are generally very small, and the emphasis on beef cattle rather than dairy farming means that there has not been the necessity to make sweeping changes in the appearance of farms by modernizing buildings; some of them still look like those in the nursery books of our childhood days. This small scale is more pronounced in the western half of the county, but even along the eastern edge adjoining Shropshire and Worcestershire it brings a contentment to the countryside and peace to the villages.

The Herefordshire border cuts across the main A49 road at Brimfield, a little place which would barely be noticed by most people passing through it if it were not for the fact that the filling station there has a thatched roof, a strange building on which to see a good example of the work of Roy Jones of Walton, near Onibury up in Shropshire. The border makes a loop which includes Little Hereford which has its church right on the bank of the River Teme. The square oasthouses among the farm buildings are a reminder that this is hop-growing country. Another sign of the hop gardens is the tall wall-like hedges, fifteen or more feet high, that are often grown as windbreaks. These are kept very neatly trimmed, and although this is a relatively easy task with the new hedge-cutting machines, it required considerable skill and agility to do it with the old-fashioned hedging tools.

Hop-growing is a specialized job and it is therefore not a crop which can be tried for a short period like many others on the farm. In this part of the country the erection of the stringing to support the vines is done with long poles like fishing rods, and working above one's head all day in this fashion is a real muscle-testing job. On a few farms, harvesting is still done in the tradi-tional way with gangs of women stripping the vines by hand, but in many hop gardens the vines are taken on trailers to hop-pick-ing machines which pull off the hops with tines.

Drying is usually supervised by experts who travel from farm to farm. The hops are spread on sacking laid over a mesh floor in the upper storey of the oasthouse and hot air is blown up from the room below. To help the hops retain their colour during the process, sulphur is burnt at the start of the drying. Very strict control of temperature throughout the period is necessary and the man in charge sleeps near the oasthouse so that he can check progress continually during the two days which it takes. No doubt there is now an electronic gadget which could do the job, but I am sure that the beer would not taste as good.

From the river the land rises quickly to the south where there are scattered farms and the small Norman church of Middleton on the Hill. Laysters, at the top, stands over 700 feet up. The village is just a straggle of cottages along the road, with the church and a large farmhouse down a lane to the south-east making a scene that seems delightfully peaceful and miles from anywhere, yet it is only five miles from Leominster.

A mile and a half from Laysters is Raddle Bank, a 1 in 7 descent, which goes down to Tenbury Wells in Worcestershire. From the top of the bank there is a view out to the valley through which the Teme flows. This is a famous fruit-growing district and the valley is filled with orchards, making it a target for a 'blossom run' in the spring, but from above it is perhaps even more striking. A romantic viewpoint is reached by a footpath across the fields from the church. This leads to Wordsworth's Stone which was set up to mark the place where the poet stood admiring the scene. It did not move him to write any great poem, perhaps because it was so quiet compared with the wild scenery of the Lake District which he knew so well.

Wordsworth's wife Mary was a Hutchinson and members of the family lived at Grantfield near Kimbolton, about midway to Leominster. Thomas Hutchinson was vicar of the parish from 1840 to 1902. In the churchyard there is a group of graves of the family—the latest when I was there being that of Miss Dorothy Wordsworth Hutchinson who died in 1972 aged 88. The village is now rapidly being built up, but the church, with a striking broach spire on its thirteenth-century tower, stands away from the changes and is reached by a lane climbing uphill, which is rather oddly signposted 'Lower Kimbolton'.

The villages of Herefordshire rarely pose round a green in the traditional way, and in most cases the cottages are scattered along a lane, being near enough for company, yet far enough apart to keep their privacy. Stoke Prior, south of the A44 road from Leominster to Bromyard is a typical example. There are a number of pleasant old black-and-white cottages, one of which is almost dwarfed by a topiary bird on a nest in its garden. I know from my own experience that box, privet and other hedging shrubs grow very quickly in the lush atmosphere of Herefordshire, and it is probably this fact which encourages people to attempt rather ambitious topiary designs, for it is possible to achieve the desired shape much more quickly than in other parts of the country. But the speedy growth also means that trimming needs to be done more frequently and some of the gardners must rue the day that they conceived the ambitious project in their garden.

The spaces between the old cottages at Stoke Prior are now being filled with modern brick houses. This is no doubt the planners' idea of a useful way of allowing more houses without extending the area of a village and thus helping to conserve the countryside, but it has the unfortunate effect of diluting the village and

taking away its atmosphere, so the scheme is of doubtful benefit.
This is particularly noticeable at the T-junction at the centre of
the village, where there is a fragment of green with the old pump,
but a modern bungalow on the bank opposite and other alterations
spoil the scene.

In many counties the churches are the centrepieces of the
villages, but in Herefordshire the church often stands apart. I've
discussed this with several vicars, but none have ever been able
to trace any reason for the position, except that in most cases
the churches are built on rising ground and it seems that they
could have been built there because this gave them more prominence, or because this was a better defensive position, while the
people of the village would tend to build their homes in more
sheltered spots.

The church at Stoke Prior is a typical example, for apart from
one large farmhouse nearby, it is the recent additions to the village
which are near to it. The path is lined with a striking avenue of
umbrella-shaped trees. The verger told me that wych elm crowns
had been grafted on to the trunks of ordinary elms, and when he
pointed them out to me I could see the joints quite clearly. The
tortured branches of the wych elms make the broad umbrella
shapes, and he said that when they were in full leaf they shed the
rain very well and protected the congregation walking up to the
church.

The church itself was very much altered in 1863, and although
this may have been thought to have been an improvement at the
time, I should have preferred the original, simpler shape which
is shown in a sketch on the wall. One alteration that must have
made people feel more comfortable was the removal of a memorial
from the church to the porch. This reads:

Under this seat lies William Cook, Elizabeth his wife and William
his grandson, who died March 15 1766. Affliction so long a time
I bore, Physicians prov'd in vain; 'Til God was pleased my grief to
ease; and free me from my pain.

Many of the Herefordshire villages are very small, but few can
be smaller than Humber which is reached down a narrow lane

along the middle of which grass and dandelions thrive. There is such a lack of any sign of activity that the traveller might give up hope of arriving anywhere if it was not for the fact that the broach spire of the church stands out so boldly as a guide. Humber is so isolated that it seems impossible that it could ever have been very populous, yet it is barely a hundred years since the church was heavily restored and a new rectory built. This has now been re-named Humber Grange and is used as a guest house. The present owner paused in the perpetual summer task of lawn-cutting to tell me of an incident which illustrates the great change in the style of life in the countryside. Not long before, one of his guests had been a lady who, as a child during the last war was evacuated to the house when it was the rectory. She had told him that although she was there for some years she had never been per-mitted even to see into any of the main rooms then; so that she had been thrilled to have the use of this 'forbidden territory' on her second visit. This makes one wonder how many townsfolk have archaic views of countryside habits based on similar experi-ences during their wartime evacuation.

Although Humber seems so isolated, every year one or two houses are built in the area; the people living in them usually having employment in town. This is one of the problems of the countryside, for if more employment is not provided in rural areas they will become little more than suburbs of the towns and the countryside will lose the atmosphere which makes it so attractive.

This atmosphere can be felt at Hatfield which lies along a little lane north of the Leominster/Bromyard road. From Hatfield Court there are farms and little groups of cottages for almost a mile and a half along a pleasantly tree-lined way. The village has the con-tentment of a self-sufficient community about it. The church fits the scene and although it has obviously been much restored it has not been spoiled to suit the ambitions of some landowner in the past, as so often happened in other villages. It is a little stone-built place with a tiny tiled bellcote. Inside there is a gallery from which the timbers of the roof and the box pews can be seen at one glance.

The church stands in peaceful surroundings overlooking a valley with sheep and Friesian cattle grazing on the slopes. It is rich, rolling countryside which is more like downland than the traditional idea of Herefordshire countryside. At one time the peace was broken by a railway from Steen's Bridge which ran along the bottom of the valley, but this has now gone and Hatfield is one place where the loss of a railway service is almost to be counted as a blessing—so long as one has alternative means of transport!

Bredenbury, in contrast, is on the busy A44 Leominster to Bromyard road, yet even there, after a showy modern start, the centre of the village lies deep amid trees near Bredenbury Court, making an oasis on the road. There I met another newcomer to the county, a village policeman who had moved down from Manchester only three years previously, but who had become so attached to the district that he was very upset at having been told that he was to be transferred to Kidderminster. This was a contradiction to those who say that the countryside is no place for modern youth, for he was no old man seeking a retreat for retirement, but a keen youngster brought up in the city who had learned to appreciate the district and the quality of life in Herefordshire. As we talked we could see the teachers in the school opposite having their after-lunch coffee on the lawn in front of the school, while some of the children were carrying out the scenery for a play they were to perform that afternoon. It was a sylvan scene which made it easy to understand the young policeman's disinclination to transfer his family to an area with the stresses and conflicts of town life.

Bredenbury has grown in importance in the last hundred years, for the older part of the school has a tablet reading 'Grendon Bishop Board School built 1874', suggesting that at that time Bredenbury was the smaller place. The church is also new, for when the local estate was sold last century the old church which had been in its grounds was demolished and a new one of surprising length built by the road. The old church of Grendon Bishop is across the fields, by Grendon Farm.

In the area between Bromyard and Tenbury Wells there are a number of small villages mostly away from the main roads. Thornbury, for instance, has only a few houses and the church standing above them. Across the far side of the churchyard there is a wonderful view across a steep little valley to Wall Hills, a 740-feet high hill with the remains of a prehistoric camp at the top.

The area seems modest enough now, but Netherwood, a mile away, is said to have been the birthplace of Robert Devereux who, after being educated at Cambridge, was taken to court by Lord Leicester. His charm won him Queen Elizabeth's favour and his courage in battle led to rapid promotion and eventually to the Earldom of Essex. Unfortunately his brilliance was accompanied by rashness and he fell into disgrace several times—once when he married the widow of Sir Philip Sidney and later when he failed in an expedition against Spain. Eventually he was appointed Lord Lieutenant of Ireland, and, like many other great figures, failed in his operations in that troubled country and was dismissed. By this time his power with the Queen had gone and on trying to raise a force to secure the dismissal of his rivals he was accused of treason and executed. Most Herefordshire families were content with local fame and the example of Essex was certainly no encouragement to them to venture into wider fields.

All along this stretch of country, the churches lie apart from the villages. In some cases the churches are now almost inaccessible. Edvin Loach church is reached by a track across the fields, while Tedstone Wafer church can only be approached by the drive of Court Farm or a path across the fields. Very little of the old church remains and most of the present building dates from 1873 although it looks even newer from the outside. This was one of the first churches in Herefordshire to be declared redundant and offered for sale for conversion to some other use.

This area has some steep slopes and valleys because it is on the eastern rim of the county and it is only a few miles across country to Shelsey Wash in Worcestershire where the famous motor hill-climbs are held. Herefordshire has few of the large mansions with their accompanying parkland which are such a feature of the Midland counties to the east, for few of the local families acquired great wealth or felt the need for building showplaces. The road leading through Tedstone Delamere, and passing the grounds of Whitbourne Hall with its grand old trees, therefore, comes as a pleasant change. The house was built for an enthusiast of the Greek revival and is based on details of the Erechtheum. As the village is approached the peaceful atmosphere is shattered by the sight of a quite large new housing estate. This seems incredible in such a rural area and is another reminder of the fact that it is only nine miles to Worcester, the estate having been built mainly to provide homes for workers in the city.

Despite this, the corner of the village by the church is little changed. Francis Godwin, who was Bishop of Hereford in the seventeenth century lived here. He is chiefly remembered for several books which he wrote including *The Man in the Moon or a Discourse of a Voyage Thither*. This is a remarkable work of imagination and foresight. It tells how, by using a team of swans which he had trained, the hero of the story rose above the earth's surface till at a great height they became immovable, showing that Godwin had foreseen that there would be a limit to the extent of the earth's gravitational pull and problems of weightlessness would arise. The hero then proved the movement of the earth and the planets and their rotation and revolution, finally going on to the moon. There he had encounters with inhabitants who lived according to their own rules and this part of the story could well have suggested the idea of *Gulliver's Travels* to Swift. The book was not published till after Godwin's death, but it was then an instant success and was translated into French by Cyrano de Bergerac. This quiet village is not the sort of place one would expect to find associated with the birth of science fiction.

Bromyard might be classed as a village in some counties, but by Herefordshire standards it is a town and it had its own Urban District Council until 1968. On the downs to the east of it is Brockhampton with a great park and an eighteenth-century red brick house, but the attraction is Lower Brockhampton House, a fourteenth-century, timber-built house with an equally noteworthy fifteenth-century gatehouse. These two properties are now owned by the National Trust.

Hidden away down the lanes by the River Frome is Avenbury, with a little church which has stood in ruins for some years. It was restored in 1881, but services have not been held in it since the early 1930s, and when it was eventually declared redundant and offered for sale in 1971, the roof was missing and walls were in such a perilous state that there were warnings that persons entering did so at their own risk. I pushed my way through the brambles to take a photograph and had a feeling that the noise of the shutter of my camera might have been sufficient to bring everything down round my ears. Yet in the road nearby I met an old parishioner who well remembered the last vicar of the church and had been at his funeral. This is a warning of the speed with which neglect can lead to the collapse of old buildings. The church was reputed to be haunted by a ghostly organist and it will be interesting to see (or hear?) if he is disturbed by the alterations and the cleaning up of the site.

There is an extreme example of the way that churches and villages are separated in Herefordshire at Stanford Bishop, which is the only church that I have found that is approached along a track through a field of currant bushes. In this case the isolation brings a splendid peace to the atmosphere of the churchyard from which there is a wide view across country to wooded hills marred only by the storage tower of a farm in the distance.

The church has a typical little bellcote and is mainly Norman and thirteenth century. Its great treasure is—or was—the chair which was said to have been carried out and placed under a tree for the use of St. Augustine when he visited the area. The story is told in a slim book *The Finding of St. Augustine's Chair* by the late James Johnston, M.B. Lond., which was written in 1889 but not published until 1898. In this he tells how in the 1830s he visited Stanford Bishop and first saw the chair, which he was told was the one in which St. Augustine had sat at his meeting with the British bishops in 603. Many years later he revisited the district

and finding that the saintly relic had been thrown aside, he purchased it. When Dr. Johnston died the chair was sent by his
executors to Canterbury where it was exhibited in the Royal
Museum and was thought by many people to be more authentic
than the Augustine Chair in the Cathedral. In 1943 a new incumbent was appointed at Stanford Bishop and he obtained the
return of the church's heirloom. Arguments arose as to the
authenticity of the chair and an expert was called in to examine
it; he gave the opinion that it was constructed of old material not
earlier than the eighteenth century. It seems that Dr. Johnston
had probably been told 'an old Sexton's tale', but it is a pity because such a relic would have been very muse-worthy.

This area is out on the eastern edge of the county where the
Malvern Hills loom up. They are often thought of as belonging
to Worcestershire, but the range is shared between the two
counties, with Worcestershire Beacon in the north and Herefordshire Beacon in the south.

The villages under the Malverns are now becoming almost
suburbs of Worcester with many new houses being erected for the
workers of that city. Cradley, however, retains a vestige of its old
self round the church which has a sundial with the motto 'Time
Tryeth Troth' which is often mentioned but not so often actually
seen. It is a very large church which was much altered in the late
nineteenth century, but it retains some of its old features, including a chest, which is over nine feet long. In the tower there is a
frame of magnificent timbers and a board dated 1795 setting a
penalty of 6d for overthrowing the bell; ringing with gloves, spur
or hat; or cursing or swearing.

Mathon has a delightful setting in park-like country with
wooded hills leading to the Malverns in the distance. Like so
many Herefordshire villages it has some intriguing surprises with
buildings of many styles. Over Cradley Brook there are more, including Town House Farm where black-and-white Friesian cows
match the magpie building. The modern traveller who merely slows
his car to look at villages like this loses much. Even those with
cameras are often so busy fiddling with adjustments that they

do not look at the subjects properly till they have the prints of transparencies. It is the custom to laugh at the Victorians who went round with sketch pads looking for 'pretty bits', but they certainly looked at the places they visited.

Colwall is a great disappointment for those who come hoping to find romantic connections with Elizabeth Barrett Browning. She was born in 1806 at Kelloe in Durham, the eldest daughter of Edward Moulton. Her father took the name of Barrett by deed poll on receiving a legacy and moved to Colwall where he built a large house in the park at Hope End. Now of course, it is impossible to think of the family part from the play *The Barretts of Wimpole Street* and it is a pity that Colwall has not survived better to give us a picture of what must have been the happy childhood of an eager young girl busy gardening, writing verse and riding in the rich countryside. When she was fifteen came the fall from her pony which injured her spine and this was followed by other tragedies. Five years later her mother died and when her father lost a great deal of his money they had to leave Hope End and went to Torquay where her brother was drowned. Most accounts treat Edward Barrett harshly, yet by the time he reached Wimpole Street he had suffered so many troubles that he deserves some sympathy. As if to foster the legend there is nothing left of the house at Hope End which was burnt down; and most of the Colwall which Elizabeth knew has also disappeared. Now the evening train brings workers returning from Worcester and there is a mineral water factory at Colwall Springs. There is nothing wrong with either commuters or mineral waters; but those who want to dream dreams at Colwall had better slip out to some of the surrounding countryside.

Further south in a dip between Ledbury and the Malverns lies Eastnor. Most Herefordshire villages have grown up slowly and naturally, but Eastnor is a creation of the nineteenth century. There is a 'medieval' castle, begun in 1812 for the first Earl Somers, which has striking angle towers, a gatehouse, and roof trusses made of iron, which was a very advanced idea at the time it was built. There is a church built by Sir Gilbert Scott in 1852 which retains the fourteenth-century tower and the memorials of some of the Cocks family, the ancestors of the Earl; and on the village green there is a well, housed in a small building which has terracotta panels by Lady Henry Somerset, daughter of the third Earl. It is a real estate village with a contrived prettiness, but time is mellowing the effect and at least those responsible were trying to create a pleasing picture.

Bosbury is a more traditional type of village. Although there is some new building, this has been kept away from the centre of the village so that the group of buildings in the street opposite the old church still remains. It is a happy mixture of half-timbered, stone and brick buildings blended by time, which is the best way to make an English village. We need places like this to remind us of the true perspective of the years. Our 'instant' age with breathless reporters gasping garbled reactions to events into microphones in a constant effort to give us immediate news could well do with a little less haste—the Prime Minister had to wait three days for news of Waterloo.

The church at Bosbury stands behind its great square detached belfry. These belfries are puzzling features, of which there are only fifty in England, seven of which are in Herefordshire. Their origin is unknown, but it is probable that some were originally built for defensive purposes, and certainly the tower at Bosbury appears to be strong enough to withstand attack, for it is twenty-nine feet square and heavily built of stone.

The cross in the churchyard is also unusual for it has retained its original head. This is said to have been spared because the village people agreed to put on it the inscription "Honour not the cross, but honour God for Christ". The cross is so tall and I am so short that I have not been able to see this but, using a tele-photo lens in a slanting light I was able to take a photograph which shows the words cut on the head.

Buried at the foot of the cross are the ashes of Mrs. Ellen Bayly who, under the pen-name Edna Lyall, wrote romantic novels which were best-sellers in Victorian days. In these she expressed her liberalism and desire for social reform which was so great that she donated her royalties for six months to a memorial for Charles Bradlaugh. Despite these leanings, Mr. Gladstone praised her *Donovan*. She used Bosbury as the setting for her novel *In Spite of All* and although she spent her last twenty years at Eastbourne, her ashes were brought to Bosbury where her brother was vicar.

Around this area there are several Fromes—Bishop's Frome, Canon Frome, Castle Frome and Halmond's Frome, which take their names from the little river Frome. They are mostly small hamlets of no particular interest, but in the church at Castle Frome there is one of the most striking fonts in the county, if not in the country as a whole—Pevsner goes so far as to say it would arrest attention in any country. The bowl is supported by writhing serpents and has carvings showing the baptism of Christ, a pair of turtle doves and the four-winged symbols of the evangelists. It is a striking lively piece of work in the typical style of the county, which is appropriate, for Castle Frome brings us to the end of this eastern border area and the next chapter deals with the more representative central part of Herefordshire.

8

Beef and Cider—
Eastern Herefordshire

S O M E counties fall neatly into areas which have their own characteristics, but the centre of Herefordshire is so homogeneous that there are no natural groupings, and it is therefore necessary to draw an arbitrary line. For this purpose the A49 road going south from Leominster to Hereford and on to Ross divides the county conveniently into eastern and western sections. It is an unlovely road and the efforts to improve it from the motorists' point of view only lead to more traffic moving more quickly so that those of us who live in the rural areas and do most of our driving in the lanes feel that we are strangers when we venture on to it. Perhaps, however, we should be grateful to the road for taking most of the through traffic so that things are more peaceful on the lesser ways.

The harsh effect that such a road has on the countryside can be seen at Hope under Dinmore where the A49 coming south from Leominster begins the climb up the wooded Dinmore Hill. The church and school are on the east of the road and the village is on the west. The church was probably sited there to have the advantage of the position on rising ground where it was also conveniently near the big house of the district, Hampton Court. The school began as a church school and was naturally placed beside the church. In the past this did not cause any difficulty for it was just a pleasant stroll from the village, but present-day traffic has become so heavy that it is dangerous to set foot on the road except for those who are very quick of wit and limb. Therefore, in the interests of safety an underpass was made to allow the children to go to school and the villagers to attend their church. Environmental planning?

The little village has some quite pleasant stone cottages and could have been a delightful place against the background of the wooded hill if it had been allowed to develop without the intrusion of the road; now it is dominated by it.

The church has a monument showing the Earl and Countess Coningsby with their infant son who is holding a cherry to mark the fact that he died in 1708 by choking on one of these small fruits. The Earl, Thomas, in this group, won royal favour at the Battle of the Boyne in 1690 where he used his handkerchief to staunch the blood of William III's wounded shoulder, but later he became involved in litigation over his estates and spent some time in the Tower as a result of some unfortunate remarks about the Lord Chancellor—an episode which also resulted in his dismissal from the Privy Council. His great-grandfather, also named Thomas, founded the Coningsby Hospital for 'Coningsby's Company of Old Servitors' in Hereford. The men used to wear scarlet coats and it is said that the famous outfit worn by the Chelsea pensioners was inspired by Nell Gwyn's memories of these.

The family lived in Hampton Court, a square-battlemented house which was refashioned in the eighteenth century, but which dates back to the fifteenth century when it was built by Sir Rowland Lenthall, who returned from Agincourt with a useful sum collected as ransom money in respect of French prisoners he had taken in the campaign. In those days profits from wars were apparently made in the front line rather than in trade at home.

The Gloucester road which turns off to the south-east here past the old house leads to more peaceful scenery than that along the main road. Bodenham sleeps along a lane and has some good old stone cottages near its centre, where, at a T-junction, there is a trim little green with a war memorial and the remnants of an old cross. Already the newer houses are blending into the scene and it makes a pleasant, if rather over-tidy picture. The church sits nicely at the end of the group with a strange lantern and a tiny spire set almost irreverently above the tower. Such traditional groupings are not typical of the county and Bodenham might almost be accused of creating a false impression of Herefordshire.

Up on the hill on the other side of the road is Pencombe which seems larger than it is because it has grown round an H-shaped junction of four lanes and has a large green sloping steeply up to the church, which appears to have been placed where it can keep an eye on things—although the village looks the sort of place where nothing untoward would occur. Yet Pencombe bred at least one really adventurous son, Richard Jordan, who, as his memorial tells, "led by a spirit of enterprise and a passionate love of Knowledge" went off on an ill-fated expedition to explore the interior of Africa when it was still the 'Dark Continent' and died there in 1832. Richard Hall, who was clerk of the parish for fifty-two years, seems to be more in keeping with the spirit of the village.

Little Cowarne is another backwater village, but it follows the more typical Herefordshire pattern of straggling along a lane through a dale. It does not look as if it could ever have been any larger or more prosperous, yet in 1870 the church was almost completely rebuilt, fortunately without any grand ideas, so it still fits this sleepy hollow. And this little haven is less than two miles from Stoke Lacy on the Bromyard/Hereford road. This is one of the secret pleasures of the county, for by using the One Inch Ordnance Survey map intelligently it is possible to find places which have an air of remoteness without having to travel miles to reach them. It is one of the few counties where you can still find peace down any lane.

Stoke Lacy, even though it is on a busy road, succeeds in preserving its rural air. True, it rebuilt its church last century and this looks as if it is waiting for some other modernities, but the village has never taken the hint and houses, barns and oasthouses, mostly built of warm red brick, have a well-loved, well-lived-in air. There are some new buildings, but most of them are tucked

I

away out of sight. One of them is the home of Madge Hooper who runs a herb farm. She is a sparkling little lady who took me on a breathless tour of garden after garden filled with plants with evocative names such as borage, basil, tarragon and dill. It was like turning the pages of *Culpepper*. I'm no gardener but I know enough to appreciate the work entailed, and the thought made me wilt. Yet Madge Hooper finds time not only to maintain the gardens but also to dry herbs, collect seeds, make jellies and give countless talks. After specializing in herbs at college she has spent thirty-seven years growing them and is interested in them as plants with a down-to-earth realism about their use. Her catalogue explains that chicory can be forced for winter salads, or its sky blue colour can be enjoyed; and orach may be cooked like spinach while its crimson leaves make it a striking foliage plant.

Up on the hill at the north end of the village is the works of Symonds, one of the three surviving cider firms in Herefordshire. Started in 1727 Symonds is still a family concern and includes fascinating drinks such as damson wine in its list.

The village was also the birthplace of Mr. Morgan whose three-wheeled cars were so well known before the last war and are still revered by those who knew them. The Morgan family restored the church organ in 1961 and I hope it has as lusty a note as the old Moggies.

Round this area, in contrast to other parts of the county, the churches are among the houses and often so tucked away that they can be easily missed. Moreton Jefferies has a tiny over-restored church dwarfed by farm buildings; and at Much Cowarne the church lies behind a farm and has to be approached by a track between barns and other buildings. Surprisingly, it is a large and well kept building with some fine monuments, including a tomb with the figures of Edmund Fox and his wife and their ten children on the side and three babes in a cradle at the end. It was no doubt a privilege to lie inside the church, but as in so many Herefordshire villages, from the churchyard, there is a magnificent view which stretches across miles of countryside to the distant hills.

The road through Stretton Grandison is being gradually improved as a way to Gloucester and this seems to have taken the heart out of the village, as most of it has been over-smartened up. Celia Fiennes, my favourite travel writer of the past, who made a number of long journeys on horseback at the end of the seventeenth century, visited New House here and it would be interesting to have her typically candid comments on the village now. The school has been converted into flats and even the church which looks attractive on its hillside site from a distance has suffered. Inside there is a rather fine memorial to Sir Edward Hopton who died in 1668 after serving Charles I "in all ye time of ye intestine troubles in many battles. . . .' He lived at Canon Frome across the Frome. The church there has now been largely rebuilt and his old home, Canon Frome Court, which was also rebuilt, has been taken over as a County Secondary School. Yarkhill along the Frome Valley has not yet taken heed of Miss Purser's discovery that it was the birthplace of Fabian Stedman of bell-ringing fame.

The road straightens out and reveals its origin as a Roman way at Ashperton. A small wayside garden has a very neatly contrived topiary horse and jockey. The owner grew a small hedge and trimmed and trained this to make a two-dimensional 'cut-out', which has since been allowed to fill out. This is an ingenious idea for those with ambitions to have some topiary work but who have not the time or patience to follow the more usual method. The church is down a lane and not so long ago could easily have been missed because of its isolation; now it may be just as easily missed because there is a building estate round it. Nearby on an island in a moat is the mound that is all that is left of the castle built by the Grandisons in the thirteenth century. They were one of the important families of the period and John, who was Bishop of Exeter from 1327 to 1369, was responsible for much of the work on the cathedral there. Now, however, it is his sister Katherine who is known by more people for she is reputed to have been the lady who lost her garter and had it returned by Edward III with the remark 'Honi soit qui mal y pense'—an incident which was the origin of the badge and motto of the Order of the Garter and became part of that 'traditional history' of England which includes King Alfred's trouble with the cakes and the Invasion of 1066.

Trumpet on the Ledbury road may appear to be only a modest place but it is famous in the county for the ploughing matches organized by its society. In Herefordshire there are many of these events and the top ploughmen of the county, such as Mr. T. L. Goodwin and Mr. J. A. Gwilliam, have achieved national fame. Every year farmers are found who are willing to put their fields at the disposal of the organizers and ploughmen gather with tractors and horses to do battle. There are classes for all styles of ploughing from the old high cut, which was used in the days when seed was broadcast by hand, to the most modern, using mounted ploughs. Compared with normal work on a farm the job is done slowly in order to get the best possible finish. It is a highly skilled craft and although it may be impractical to work to such a high standard, the skills which are learned for competition work also result in better ploughing in normal conditions.

Those who have a sentimental regard for the 'good old days' but no experience of working with a horse, will be surprised by the hurry and flurry of the horse teams with the ploughman struggling along behind trying to control horses and plough at the same time; in comparision the tractor drivers appear to work leisurely. I learnt this lesson when I first left London and went as a trainee on a farm. In those days of 1949 there were still some working horses and some of my most hair-raising days were spent helping to horse-hoe root crops. Prince, the old horse, seemed to have eight huge feet and his pace was just a little too fast for Dick and I so that at the end of the day we felt we had spent the time racing across the uneven ground of the field.

Around Trumpet there are a number of small villages including Munsley, Pixley and Aylton, the last of which is one of those corners which are remembered when many more famous places have become confused memories. There is a cluster of cottages, a farm with a grand old timber-built barn and, set on a small mound, a tiny church with a bell turret. Inside, the walls are leaning, the screen is an assembly of old work and there is a fine air of age and homeliness. This is a church which belongs to the countryside.

Even deeper in the maze of lanes at Putley Green, the village hall, post office and a cottage gather to make a picture which is unusually traditional for the county.

Much Marcle along the road to Ross is larger than most of the places in this area. The big houses, Hellens, Homme House and Hall Court indicate its past importance, and this is also reflected in the church which is approached through lych-gates formed by yew trees. In the lofty building there are many memorials including a striking seventeenth-century tomb chest with the figures of Sir John Kyrle and his wife, and the charmingly realistic figure of Lady Blanche Grandison from the fourteenth century in a recess.

Now however, these stone figures are rather put out of face by a wooden one, said to be of Walter de Helyon, a fourteenth-century yeoman. For many years Walter was painted a stone colour, but in 1971 he was borrowed by the authorities at the London Museum for an exhibition 'Chaucer's London'. While he was there, experts removed the stone-coloured paint and restored it to what is believed to be its original colours of 700 years ago. Walter is dressed in a short, tight-fitting tunic with a short sword in his belt, and now adds a brave touch of colour to the church.

Much Marcle is a centre of the cider industry. From the seventeenth century, Herefordshire farmers had sold their surplus cider to merchants in Ledbury, who had sent it down the Severn to Bristol, from where it was shipped round the coast to London and the North. This trade began to fall off in the nineteenth century when cider-making on farms was reduced owing to the grubbing up of many orchards to meet the shortage of grain caused by the Napoleonic Wars.

In the second half of the nineteenth century, Mr. C. W. Ratcliffe Cooke of Hellens, Much Marcle, M.P. for Hereford, advocated the value of cider as a national beverage so strongly that he was nicknamed 'The Member for Cider'. His efforts encouraged a number of people in the county to start cider-making factories; among them was Henry Weston, then tenant of the Bounds at Much Marcle, who thought that it would be a useful business to add to his fifty-acre farm. The firm has now become one of the best-known makers of cider, and the rural nature of its background is maintained by the yard of Hereford cattle in front of the offices. The factory set up on a hill above the village looks out across the countryside which produces the apples it uses. Although machines are used in the factory the process is very similar to that used on the farms. The firm now provides a useful source of employment in the village and as the men are all able to do several tasks, by moving them round from job to job according to the season, they are given full employment.

In the south-west, Herefordshire comes up to the hills of the Forest of Dean and the Gloucestershire border. Here lies Weston under Penyard which likes to be known as the garden village of south Herefordshire. Bollitree Castle is a quite normal seventeenth-century building with a wide range of outbuildings which have battlements and towers, some of which came from Penyard Castle, of which there were scant remains about two miles away—but even these are not marked on the latest map.

From Upton Bishop and Linton which stand on high ground to the east of Ross on Wye there are striking views of the county towards Hereford and some of the many twists and turns of the Wye can be seen. The B4224 follows the line of the river but rarely gives a sight of it. Herefordshire, despite its lush growth of grass and shrubs, does not as a rule have very impressive trees, but along this stretch of valley there are some of the best; indeed How Caple Grange, now a hotel, is so buried in trees that it is almost impossible to see the very handsome chimneys.

Many of our churches have interesting features from the past and most of them have the marks of the Victorians; if we do not always appreciate their efforts, at least they did what they felt was best. It is unusual to see anything done since the turn of the century, but in the church down by How Caple Court a seventeenth-century screen with the arms of William III is now complemented by some good woodwork added by the Lee family in the 1920s.

Here the Wye makes one of its great loops. It is only a mile and a half by road to Brockhampton, yet it is nine miles along the river bank. The village truly merits the description 'lost in the lanes' because it dawdles along narrow lanes for such a distance that it is very difficult to say where it ends. Here is an example of twentieth-century additions to our treasury of churches, for there is one of the newest in the county, built in 1901–2 by Mrs. Alice Madeline Forster as a memorial to her parents, Eben D. and Julia Jordan of Massachussetts This is a striking effort to create something new rather than following the lines of convention. Even from the outside the church strikes a strange note with its tower, wooden belfry and thatched roof; inside it is unlike any other, with deep arches rising from comparatively low walls creating a vault-like effect. That the church is still cared for is shown by the fact that in 1952 canvas covers were made for the hymn books and these were embroidered with the English wild flowers which are the theme of the carvings decorating the choir stalls.

Sollers Hope is the first of a little group of 'hope' villages— this name, indicating a settlement in a valley, is more frequently found in Shropshire than in Herefordshire. Fownhope is becoming overbuilt with modern houses but still manages to retain the pleasant air of a typical valley village. An old milestone outside the church states, probably inaccurately owing to road alterations, that it is '$6\frac{1}{4}$ miles and 56 yards' to Hereford. The church itself is large for such a small village, being 119 feet long, and it has a tall broach spire which is said to have 22,000 oak shingles on it. At one time Fownhope must have been a place of some importance, but there is little sign of this now. The most famous son of the village was Thomas Winter, born in 1795, who for professional purposes took the younger sounding name of Tom Spring and became a famous pugilist. After Tom Cribbs retired in 1821, Spring became acknowledged as the 'Champion of All England'. He was landlord of a public house in London and apparently did very well out of fighting—and in his days it was real fighting, for one battle at the race-course at Worcester lasted seventy-seven rounds before he was declared victor. He returned to the county and for a time was landlord of the 'Booth Hall' at Hereford where there is a portrait of him, but he later went back to London where he had the 'Castle Tavern', Holborn.

Up in the hills behind is Woolhope, a name which has become familiar because of the activities of the Woolhope Naturalists Field Club. Founded in 1851, this club has attained a great reputation. The members were at first mainly interested in the geology of the hills in this area where there was a great landslip in 1575 (the site is marked on the Ordnance Survey Map), but over the years their interests have widened and many questions of local history have been investigated. The results have been published in a series of volumes which are now a mine of information on the county, although they tend to include many smaller issues. The volumes themselves are becoming of historical interest as the earlier ones have accounts of expeditions in the days before the motor car and have a quaint almost Pickwickian air about them.

The manor of Woolhope was originally owned by Lady Godiva and her sister Wulviva, who gave it to Hereford Cathedral, a fact that is commemorated by a modern window in the church which has pictures of the two sisters and the famous nude ride.

A road through Haugh Wood drops down to Mordiford which has a little bridge over the Lugg just before it joins the Wye. The Hereford family had to keep a close watch on this bridge because they held the manor on condition that they presented the King with a pair of gilt spurs every time he rode over it. This may not seem a likely royal route nowadays, but at the time when Ludlow and other border castles were occupied this would have been a much more important road.

Mordiford now makes a pretty picture with its stone-built cottages at the foot of the wooded hills, but it has not always been so peaceful. In 1811 a thunderstorm turned the little Pentaloe brook into a raging torrent, twenty feet deep and a hundred and eighty feet wide, which brought down rocks, swept away buildings and drowned four villagers. The story was told on

Black-and-white at Weobley

The massive detached
belfry at Bosbury

The pagoda-like detached
belfry at Pembridge

Clun church has a typical border-style tower

Culmington spire is topped with aluminium fins

The Italian-style campanile above Hoarwithy

At Eardisley a barn has been converted into homes

Brook House and its dovecot at King's Pyon

Old church at Llanwarne

New Catholic church at Ewyas Harold

Luntley Court—the dovecot and cottages

The church at Staunton is well above the Arrow

a board in the church porch, but this is now illegible. The church
has also lost its central tower and a twelve-feet long dragon which
was painted on the outside. In 1973, to celebrate the centenary
of their school, the local children staged a pageant portraying the
battle between the Green and Red Dragons, which ended when the
Red Dragon decided to stay in the west and became the figure on
the flag of Wales, and the Green Dragon was converted and became
the picture on the church. According to another story the dragon
had been threatening the local people and was killed by a condemned criminal. Unfortunately the prosaic truth is thought to
be that the dragon was part of the arms of the Priory of St.
Guthlac.

Mordiford has also lost its vicar, but Hampton Bishop, just
across the bridge in the marshy land between the Wye and the
Lugg, is prospering; for being only three miles from the centre of
Hereford it has attracted much new building. This has changed the
character of the village but it is benefiting the church and when
I met the vicar he was very pleased with the support he was
getting. The half-timbered upper part of the church tower and its
shingled roof combine with a nearby thatched cottage to make
a camera-attracting group that have earned an 'olde worlde' reputation for the village.

The road from Mordiford continues around the foot of the
Woolhope Hills through a pleasant string of villages. The first of
these is Dormington with some of the largest hop gardens in the
county which are surrounded by very high hedges, indicating
the strength of the wind in the area. Next is Stoke Edith where the
church and the big house were built by the Foleys. Now the big
house is only a shell, for it was burnt down in 1927, but the
church remains as the family rebuilt it and has an imposing
memorial to Paul Foley, who died in 1699. At Tarrington, the
'Foley Arms' is a further reminder of this old family, but nowadays the name of the village is better known for the herds of
Herefordshire cattle in the area.

Lugwardine is fast becoming a suburb of Hereford, but Withington by the Hereford to Worcester road is a delightful place. Where

the lane to the village leaves the main road, the remains of an old cross were converted into a milestone in 1700 and distances to Hereford, Worcester and Ledbury can still be read on the stone, which is known locally as the 'White Stone'. The village itself is a pleasant surprise, for after the many dispersed communities in the county it is a change to find one so comfortably set round a green, with the church and its slender spire at the end.

Sutton St. Nicholas and Sutton St. Michael are almost joined now, so that only the inhabitants can tell where the borderline is, but in the past there was the rivalry which could be expected between two such neighbours. Sutton St. Nicholas is the larger place with some medieval farms and cottages round its church, which is also the bigger, although not so interesting. Sutton St. Michael on the other hand, belonged originally to the Benedictine monastery in Hereford and later to the Knights Hospitallers of St. John. After the Dissolution it passed into the hands of the Lingen family who were Catholics and suffered as a result of the support they gave the King in the Civil War. Later, St. Michael became a poor living and for some time had to make do with a stipendary curate who also served as curate to the rector of Sutton St. Nicholas, which could not have been a very happy situation for the parishioners. Now the two benefices have been united, but the local loyalties still persist.

Above the two Suttons is Sutton Walls Camp which was occupied in Iron Age times and until Saxon days. Now it is the cause of much local controversy because of a dump there which causes a nuisance. It is believed to have been the site of the castle to which Ethelbert, King of East Anglia, came to ask for the hand of Offa's daughter, Alfrida, in 794. There are various accounts of what happened, but most agree that Queen Quendra instigated events which led to Ethelbert's murder. The body was first buried by the Lugg, and it was later taken up and reburied in Hereford. At the site of the first burial a spring appeared, the water of which was claimed to have healing properties. There the church at Marden was built. Nothing survives of the early church, and the present building dates from the thirteenth century although it has been much rebuilt. In the floor is the well of St. Ethelbert which has been dry for some years. Despite its antiquity the church has a modern look which is emphasized by the fact that there are no tombstones near the church. This is not due to modern tidying up but to an Order in Council of 1899 forbidding burials in that area of the churchyard on account of public health. This may have been due to the vulnerability of the site to flooding, for as recently as 1947 the church was flooded to the depth of eighteen inches.

The Vern, Marden, was the home of the world famous Vern herd of Herefordshire cattle which had a great influence on the breed. The two great periods of the herd were from 1850 to 1873, when John Hewer was there, and from 1922 to 1965 when Captain R. S. de Q. Quincey owned it. Hewer's cattle traced back to a white-faced bull born in 1797 and it was their success which mainly set the colour markings with the white face so familiar today. Captain de Q. Quincey in his turn changed the shape of the breed, for he bred the smaller, quicker-maturing cattle which are known today. Animals from the Vern won prizes as far away as Australia and the Argentine.

Away to the west is Preston Wynne, where at Rosemaund the Ministry of Agriculture has an experimental farm, which does work on a national programme and also on matters of special local interest, including sheep and cattle rearing and hop cultivation. Rosemaund did some very interesting work on the in-wintering of sheep with the idea of "providing the shepherd with easier working conditions". This sounded an appealing idea, for when I was on farms I often acted as unofficial shepherd's mate and although I must confess that I enjoyed those days there were occasions when we would have liked to have avoided the task of plodding round fields that were deep in mud looking for the lamb that had lost its ewe and vice versa. On the other hand sheep are by nature such creatures of the hilltops and moorlands that they looked wrong confined to sheds.

At Moreton on Lugg a large supply depot has led to much

modern building, but it still retains a delightfully ancient and horribly narrow bridge.

On the other side of the A49, just south of Dinmore Hill, is Wellington, reached by a maze-like course through lanes. This is a quite superior sort of village for Herefordshire, as it has a pavement and the buildings are concentrated along a street. They are the usual local mixture of all types and another demonstration of the fact that harmony is the important factor in creating a good village. Particularly striking are some of the weatherboarded barns; and opposite the church is an octagonal dovecot which is in surprisingly good condition inside, with the nest boxes well preserved despite the fact that it was being used as a storeplace when I last saw it.

On the northern outskirts of Hereford is Holmer, now nearly swallowed up by the city. This has one of the seven detached belfries in Herefordshire, although there is now a lean-to building between it and the church. The possible defensive purpose of the tower is indicated by its strong base, which is crowned by a half-timbered top.

The last section of this chapter covers the area south of Hereford between the Wye and A49; barriers ancient and modern. This is a delightfully forgotten part of the county with lanes that wander round and over hills that are often striking because of the way that they suddenly thrust upwards, despite being of no very great height.

Along the B4399 from Hereford is poor Rotherwas chapel which has suffered so greatly. There was an Ordnance Factory there during the war and now there is a dump. The eighteenth-century Rotherwas House has been demolished and the little chapel is marooned in a wasteland, surrounded by a high wire fence and 'done up' by the Department of the Environment in its best style. The little churchyard is beautifully mown and the outside of the building repointed and repainted so that it has the meretricious air of a model church ready to drop into a toy village.

The area seems to have an attraction for military minded people. There is an Iron Age Hill fort on the top of Dinedor Hill nearby, and during the siege of Hereford in 1645, the forces camped there. In the lea of the hill is Dinedor, which has now been nearly submerged in new building that has not yet blended into the scene. The church promises better things. It clings to the old name of Dyndor and is delightfully situated down a long path from the road so that it appears to be detached from the changes which have occurred. In fact it suffered its own change last century and only the west tower is original, but it still makes a pleasing picture to remember.

The Herefordshire School of Agriculture dominates Holme Lacy. Everything is spick and span, modern and very businesslike; although in 1972–73, 7,000 students attended full and part-time courses, the school made a profit of nearly £14,000 on its 500-acre farm; a tribute to the standard of management, for the requirements of teaching do not always coincide with good farming.

Holme Lacy was granted to the Lacys after the Conquest and passed to the Scudamores through marriage. The great days began when John Scudamore acquired considerable wealth at the time of the Dissolution of the Monasteries, and it was then that the great house was built. The family's influence continued to grow and a later John, the first Viscount, was ambassador in Paris. However, during the Civil War he was imprisoned for several years and the great house was only saved by the intervention of General Wall, a Puritan, but a gentleman. On his release Lord Scudamore devoted himself to agriculture and especially fruit-growing. He was the first to classify the apples used in cider-making and introduced the famous Red Streak Pippin—work which has made his name the toast of Hereford's cider drinkers.

Now the great house is used as a mental hospital and to see how great the Scudamores were it is necessary to go down the narrow little lane that leads to the old church tucked away by the river. At first sight this appears to be just a small village church with a squat tower, but inside the tunnel vaulting and the massive piers separating it into a nave and south aisle of almost equal size give it a cavernous appearance. The nave, furnished with plain benches, has an air of simplicity contrasting with the huge marble and alabastar monuments to Scudamores from the sixteenth century onwards. There are great table tombs with figures, and elaborate wall monuments surrounded with drapery and cherubs. The low roof makes them all seem rather over-size, creating an imposing impression of the glories of the family.

There is also departed glory at Aconbury, which lies in delightful wooded hill country a few miles west. Among a scatter of farms and buildings is a church which has always been as unpretentious as it is now, but which was built as the church of a house of the Sisters of St. John of Jerusalem in the thirteenth century. When I visited the church in 1973 I found workmen busy pulling creeper off the walls and making sure that the fabric was sound; but inside all was desolate, for the building was officially closed. The wall paintings were faded and the chancel was being used as a storeplace for items removed from redundant churches. Fonts from Mansell Gamage, Brobury, Avenbury and other churches stood there with only roughly written cards to identify them. Perhaps at some time the church will be made into a museum to show these pieces off, but at present there are no plans for this.

The next villages south each have delightful surprises. The first is Little Dewchurch which looks nice enough in a quiet sort of way as it is approached along the road from Aconbury. The speeding tourist no doubt nods and passes on, but the heart of the village lies along the side road by the school. This leads past old cottages and then to a hollow bowl with the old church ringed by a farm and old buildings making a delightfully cosy picture.

At neighbouring Hoarwithy the road drops steeply down a wooded hillside with the promise of a picture-type English village; but instead there are whitewashed stone buildings, with a little stream running down to the Wye, which have a Welsh air; while high above the village on a shoulder is a great campanile which could have come from southern Italy. In 1843 Hoarwithy had built itself a neat brick church, but this was not grand enough for William Poole who went as vicar forty years later, so he added this striking tower and an equally imposing chancel. The original nave retains its simplicity, but the chancel has four great marble columns rising up to a dome. A mosaic floor, marble altar and richly carved choir stalls add a richness which perhaps satisfied the vicar but is in dramatic contrast to the village below.

Over the river on a hilltop, caught in a great loop of the Wye, is Kings Caple which although it seems inaccessible, has quite a number of new houses. However it retains Caple Court and some old farms standing guard round its simple church. A note inside says that "the chancel is unrestored, all vestiges of antiquity are hidden beneath plaster of the fourteenth century". Time may run slowly in Herefordshire, but it is surely extreme to regard the four-teenth century as modern.

Kings Caple seems a friendly place, perhaps because it is one of the three villages in the area with the custom of giving Pax Cakes on Palm Sunday. This is believed to have started with a bequest by a Lady Scudamore of the sixteenth century. The round, flat cakes are stamped with the Lamb and Flag, the emblem of St. John the Baptist, to whom Kings Caple church is dedicated. Now the cakes are handed out by the vicar at the end of the service with the words "Peace and Good Neighbourhood", but originally old enemies were expected to break and share a cake at the church door and thus end their dispute. The other two churches at which this custom is observed are at Sellack and Hentland. Sellack is little more than a hamlet at the end of a lane that sidles down a wooded slope to the Wye, so hidden away that, in spite of its high steeple, the church cannot be seen from far away. Hentland is equally hidden down a lane and looks as if it must always have had a modest existence, but it was at one time quite important. There is a clue in the churchyard in a very worn cross head that shows the figure of Christ on one side and that of Saint Dubricius on the other. The saint, to whom the church is dedicated, is one of those shadowy figures of border mythology who is said to have crowned King Arthur and at Hentland he is believed to have set up a college, but there is no sign of this now.

All the better villages are away from the main road in this area. Along the main Hereford to Ross road there are Much Birch,

Llandinabo and Peterstow, but they have little of interest. It is much more rewarding to travel to Foy which is at the end of a road which goes out into a great narrow loop of the Wye. As it becomes narrower and more penned in by hedges no doubt many travellers wish that they had heeded the warning of the 'No Through Road' sign; then the river is sighted and suddenly Foy itself. In spite of its position it is larger than most of the villages in the area, and although it is in the heart of the country it has the air of a coastal village. Perhaps this is due to the whitewashed cottages and houses with bright flowers in their gardens, or perhaps a breeze manages to snake its way along the valley. The church is a surprise too, larger and more imposing than would be expected with many memorials to the Abrahalls, one of whom in 1640 bequeathed lands, goods and stocks to pay for a "fayer windowe contayning three lights and there place the same after the same manner as such a window placed in the church at Sellack".

Such a pleasant, end-of-the-road place makes an appropriate ending to this chapter.

9

Into the Mountains—
South-West Herefordshire

THE area south-west of Hereford includes a great diversity of countryside, from the quiet villages of the central plain and the peace of the upper Wye Valley to the hills in the south-west that lead up to the Black Mountains. There are no towns in the area as can be seen on the map which shows the villages scattered evenly over the countryside rather than being in groups round centres like iron filings in a magnetic field. Yet in the past the area had its times of importance. At Kenchester there was the most important Roman centre in the county; Peterchurch had a stone church when Hereford still had only a building of timber, wattle and daub; and there was the great Dore Abbey. This could be an area living on its past glories, looking back regretfully at days gone by; instead it is a place where time is forgotten, where life runs easily and the little courtesies can be observed. Where else in August 1973 would have happened an incident typical of many which helped to make the writing of this book such a pleasure? I was chasing a fleeting sun with my camera and stopped at a little village shop to buy some bread and cheese to make a snack so that I could carry on with as short a break as possible. As she took the money the lady asked if I had a knife and I told her that I could manage with my pocket knife. Oh no! That would never do. She went behind the scenes to get her bread knife and proceeded to slice the loaf for me. She knew that it was most

K

unlikely that I would call at the shop again; it was just a little
kindness that made a day feel better.

This peaceful atmosphere begins quite close to Hereford. Less
than four miles from the city along the Abergavenny road is
Allensmore, lying quietly among a maze of lanes so that it is
difficult to estimate its size. Near the church there is a happy
mixture of half-timbered and brick cottages with several fine
farmhouses. By the porch in the churchyard is a weatherworn
stone which shows a blacksmith at his forge; it's a nice place
that lays a blacksmith in such a privileged position. And although
Winnals and Thruxton are now almost joined together, with
many new houses, there is a pleasant corner where the church
stands on a small rise by an old mound and a large farm.

The collection of carvings in the church at Kilpeck is one of
the most well-known tourist targets in the country. The church
is small and simple with a nave, chancel and apse, a pattern
found in a number of others in the district. However, the wealth
of carvings holds the eye so firmly that little else is noticed. Other
places have one or two treasured carvings, but Kilpeck has almost
a riot of them. The south doorway has two soldiers in peaked
caps on the shafts, a Tree of Life on the tympanum and a strange
collection of animals and figures on the outer line of the arch.
Even more fascinating are the figures on the corbel table round the
building. These are worthy of careful study, for they are full of
variety and detail. There are strange heads, a fiddler, and animals
and figures, some of which amazingly foreshadow the creations
of Walt Disney. They are a strange decoration on a church, for
many seem to have little relevance to the Christian message, but
they must have given the villagers of Kilpeck a special affection
for their church over the years. The carvings on the interior are
rather more restrained, but the chancel arches have the figures of
three apostles one above the other and even the stoup is clasped
round with two arms, making it look like a corpulent stomach.

The village itself receives less attention, yet it provides the
perfect setting for the church. The pleasant green by the church,
now partially taken for a car park, the farm and the quiet cottages

nearby create the perfect atmosphere. In some counties the gardens would be full of plastic gnomes and there would be a gift shop selling replicas of the sheila-na-gig on the corbels.

In complete contrast, Much Dewchurch is traditional, with the high Victorian pyramid roof of the church standing out prominently as the village is approached. The local big house is the Mynde, which may go back to the sixteenth century, and there are a number of memorials to the families that have held it. Walter Pye, who was Attorney General to James I, is shown kneeling with his wife, while underneath their many children are ranged in sexes. The sculptor gave them a much stronger family resemblance than is usual. There is a typically Victorian conceit on the memorial to Richard Harcourt Symons who died in 1850, which shows a woman seated sorrowfully below a weeping willow tree.

Even in such a peaceful area there are troubles, as can be seen at Llanwarne which lies pleasantly in the valley of the little Gamber brook. On a summer day this looks a pleasant valley village with tall trees, comfortable stone buildings and the Gamber trickling through the scene, which is spoilt only by the sight of the old church standing in ruins. This is not another case of a decayed parish. In winter the Gamber would gather enough water to flood the site and the old church was abandoned in 1864 and a new one built on higher ground across the road. The old church now has no roof, there is grass growing along the top of the walls and nettles crowding the interior. The old arches still stand firm, a tribute to the early builders, but this is a warning of what can happen to a church which is left to look after itself. The old font has been taken up to the new church and the pulpit also looks as if it has been transferred. Churches in Herefordshire are usually built on high ground and it is surprising that this error should have been made at Llanwarne.

Neighbouring Pencoyd certainly avoided the mistake and, as a sergeant during the war advised us, made sure to keep its feet dry. Llangarron is also built on a slope and lies above the Garren Brook. Although it is quite large it was a sleepy place on the hot

summer day when I last visited it and even the large dog on guard
on the steps of the post office did not bother to lift his head as I
went past. Llangarron is unique in having a sundial on top of its
steeple, but this is not so futile as it sounds, for when the tip of
the steeple was replaced the old stones were erected in the churchyard to form the base of a sundial. The church has been very
much restored but it has retained a flagon presented to it in the
seventeenth century by William Gwillym who has a very handsome monument in the chancel—a huge tablet with cherub's
heads, scrolls and flowers, which looks like a Victorian valentine
card.

St. Weonards stands on the crest of a hill on the Hereford/
Monmouth road with the church and its great square tower at the
top beside a large farm. Little is known of the saint from whom
the village takes its name and to whom the church is dedicated
One seventeenth-century visitor to the church recorded seeing in
a window a picture of an old man with a book in one hand and
an axe in the other; while another early visitor saw the picture
of an old hermit in the same window. Unfortunately, the window
disappeared some time ago, but the accounts of it confirm (or
perhaps started?) the tradition that the saint was a woodcutter
and a hermit. Despite the belief in his humble status there was a
local legend that he was buried in a gold coffin in the mound near
the church. When this was opened in 1855, however, only two
burnt burials were found—and no gold-encased St. Weonard.
In the church there are a number of memorials to the Mynors
family who have held Treago Castle since the early fourteenth
century. The castle lies in the valley below the village and although
it has been much altered over the years, especially in the nineteenth century, it is an impressive looking building with round
towers at the corners.

From the castle, the land rises up to the hills overlooking the
Monmow valley with Orcop on a shoulder and Garway along
Garway Hill. There are a number of outlying hamlets including
Garway Common where the school is situated, and where there is
a cricket pitch mown on the village green. Down below, in Garway

'proper', is the little church of St. Michael which is one of the six churches in England attributable to the Knights Templars, to whom it was given in the twelfth century. Traces have been found of the foundations of a round church, a style favoured by the Order because it was the shape of the Church of the Holy Sepulchre in Jerusalem. In 1308 the church passed into the hands of the Knights of St. John of Jerusalem. There is such a remote air about the present church that it is difficult to associate it with these historical facts, but fortunately, like a voice from the past, there is an inscription over the door of the dovecot in the adjoining farm to the effect that it was built by Brother Richard in 1326. There is some argument as to whether this merely records a rebuilding, but to me it is Brother Richard himself who is most important, for he is a fact in a haze of conjecture.

The present church is made particularly striking by its west tower which is about thirty-three feet square and seventy feet high. When first built this was one of Herefordshire's detached towers, but it is now joined to the nave by a short corridor erected in the seventeenth century. It was originally built for defensive purposes but it was put to other uses and the ground floor is still known locally as the 'prison'.

Along the way to Welsh Newton there is a fine view of Pembridge Castle standing out in the hillside ahead, marred only by its 'frame' of two giant electricity towers and the three lines of wires they carry. The thirteenth-century castle has been restored and altered over the centuries for use as a private house, but it still looks impressive from the outside with its round towers and gatehouse. John Kemble who was hanged in 1679 for saying mass at the castle is buried in the churchyard at Welsh Newton, a small valley village on the Monmouth road.

The far south of the county here includes the stretch of the Wye Valley through Symonds Yat, and is also cut by the A40 trunk road, so that it suffers from both hurrying tourists and fast lorries. Walford has one or two good large houses, but I mostly remember it for the view of the castle at Goodrich across the river. This is a grand, powerful-looking place with impressive walls rising from the rock, so that it seems to have grown rather than being built, for it is of the same red sandstone. It is an ancient site, mentioned first under the name of Godric's Castle, but the present keep which probably dates from about the middle of the twelfth century is the oldest part now standing. On the north and west the castle is protected by a steep slope, while on the other sides there is a wide moat. This is one of the few castles which still *looks* like a castle.

The dramatically poised ruin and the striking views of the river in the district have created a romantic air in which the fantastic flourishes. When Wordsworth visited Goodrich he was annoyed by the sight of Goodrich Court, a nineteenth-century Gothic castle. This has now been demolished but in the village, 'Ye Hostelrie' with an abundance of turrets and pinnacles, is said to have been inspired by a picture in a missal. It is what would now be called 'a fun thing' or 'in bad taste' according to one's point of view. Nearby, Newhouse Farm, built in 1636, is another curio erected in three ranges placed radially, possibly to represent the idea of the Holy Trinity, as was intended in Sir Thomas Tresham's Triangular Lodge at Rushton in Northamptonshire.

Goodrich has had colourful characters to match its architectural extravagances. Dean Swift's grandfather, Thomas, was rector in the seventeenth century at the church up on the hill opposite the castle. Unlike the vicar of Bray who trimmed his sails to the prevailing wind, Swift was an ardent Royalist and is reputed to have done his part to help the cause—even to putting spiked iron balls in the river to maim the Parliamentary cavalry when they crossed. Later when Charles I was at Raglan Castle after Naseby, he went there and offered the King his waistcoat, and as this had 300 sovereigns sewn in the lining it proved to be very acceptable. As a result of these activities he was imprisoned for some time, which was rather better treatment than that handed out to many others who became engaged in the struggle.

Goodrich does have some more respectable memories. Besides becoming cross about Goodrich Court, Wordsworth is said to have met the little girl of his poem 'We are Seven' there. I am cautious about this because I see that the claim has been disputed. And buried in the churchyard is Joshua Cristall, who was one of the founders of the old Water Colour Society; some of his paintings are in Hereford Art Gallery.

Poor Whitchurch and Ganarew are now overshadowed by the A40 trunk road and its constant stream of lorries and other speeding traffic. At Welsh Bicknor, the childhood home of Henry V, both the old house and the church have been modernized.

The border follows the Monmow here and the castles at Skenfrith and Grosmont on the Monmouthshire side give an indication of the unfriendly relations in the past. There was a fourteenth-century castle at Kentchurch, but this was largely rebuilt by Nash at the beginning of the nineteenth century, and it is now a country house standing in a deer park. It is difficult to associate the present peaceful scene with the stormy past; or with the sorrow of Alice, one of Owain Glyndwr's daughters, who married Sir John Scudamore and was to hear that he and their three sons had been executed after the battle of Mortimer's Cross in 1461.

North-west of Kentchurch the boundary makes a loop to the Black Mountains and takes in a cluster of little villages in a network of steep lanes between hills that reach the 1,000 feet mark. Rowlstone, perched on the slope of a hillside, has an old Norman church with some of the best examples of the work of the Herefordshire school of carvers, including a number of birds. This motif is found on Rowlstone's most famous possessions, two iron candle brackets, each fifty-five inches long with space for five candles, and a decoration of birds alternating with fleurs-de-lis. The birds on the two brackets differ and perhaps, on the evidence of their tails, are swans and cocks.

Nearer the border, on a hillside, is Walterstone, with the church and the mound of an old castle close together, a pattern which is found at a number of places on this western side of the county. There was a Roman settlement nearby and the remains of an Iron Age hill fort and a Bronze Age barrow show that through many centuries this position above the junction of the Ewyas and the Monmow was considered important. Now that the days of conflict are over, Walterstone has become just a quiet village with glorious views of the Monmouthshire mountains.

A narrow road round Mynydd Merddin drops steeply down to Clodock which seems like an oasis of peace in the valley. St. Clodock was a grandson of King Brychan of Brecknockshire, who is reputed to have had forty-nine children all brought up as missionaries—one way of spreading the gospel. His church, tucked between the road junction and the river and approached by an old stone slab stile, is a surprise, because instead of being the expected small hill type it has a long, very broad and tall Norman nave and a good three-decker pulpit and panelled pews.

Higher up the valley where the rivers Escley, Olchon and Monmow join up is Longtown, which merits its name for it climbs for some distance up the shoulder of a hill to the remains of its castle. The line of the Offa's Dyke Long Distance path goes along the top of the Black Mountain, which stands impressively to the west, and in Longtown there is an Adventure Centre run by the Northampton County Borough Council. To the young folk from the other side of England, even in these days the countryside must seem very remote and unfriendly. The road follows the river Monmow into the hills, eventually discovering Craswall which is separated from its old Priory by about a mile. Tucked away near the Welsh border with hills all around it is completely unlike the popular picture of green and gentle Herefordshire. By its church is a square pit said to have been used for cock fights.

The importance that this border area held in the past is demonstrated again at Ewyas Harold in the Dore Valley, for this had one of the earliest Norman castles in England, built by Osbern Pentecost before the Norman invasion. In 1120 a priory was founded nearby.

All this seems very far away in present-day Ewyas Harold, a comfortable place busy about its own business, where the Dulas Brook wends its way among stone cottages. Perhaps it was the very peace of the situation which led to its fall from grace? For by the middle of the fourteenth century, the Abbot complained that monks sent to Ewyas for even short periods were so debased that they corrupted their fellows when they returned. It is a pity that fuller details are not available. Ewyas could never have been a hotbed of crime and lust; perhaps what was meant was that the monks became afflicted with Herefordshire *laissez-faire* and lost their sense of discipline.

The castle did not last much longer than the priory. In 1403 the owners were empowered to refortify it against Owain Glyndwr, but then it declined and by the time of Henry VIII it was reported to be in ruins.

Now there is no trace of the priory—most of the stones of the castle have been taken for building barns and other useful structures—and of the great people, the most striking reminder is the very flat figure of a lady in a recessed tomb in the church who is said to be Lady Clarissa, daughter of John Tregoz, Lord of Ewyas, who died in 1290. So there remained just the church, the cottages and the brook and these have continued to keep company, adthough now they have been joined by the John Kemble Catholic Church, very modern in style and not in the least what one would expect to find in a village.

The road from Ewyas skirts round the hill and then runs beside the River Dore through the Golden Valley; this probably took its name from the river but is rather unfortunate because it leads visitors to expect rather more than is there. It is pleasant, but no more than many other valleys in the county.

Dore Abbey was founded in the twelfth century by a Lord of Ewyas and in the following century it became a grand place with monastic quarters and a church 250 feet long. All this glory was ended by the Dissolution and afterwards it fell into such a bad state of repair that cattle sheltered among the stones. Dore Abbey might have continued to decay and become just another ruin to be rescued by the Department of the Environment, but about 1633 Lord Scudamore, whose family had benefited from the Dissolution, set about doing something to put the record right by restoring the old building. John Abel, the famous Herefordshire carpenter and architect, was engaged to do the job and he made a new village church from the crossing, transepts and chancel of the old abbey.

Among the additions was a great wooden screen with columns, a cornice and coats of arms and obelisks along the top. Recently it has acquired a new fame from the festivals held there. It is a difficult building to look at, because one does not know whether to consider it as a relic of the old abbey, preserved by the rebuilding of the roof, or as a village church of very lofty and strange proportions.

Buried in the church is John Hoskyn who died in 1638. He was a lawyer who spent a period in the Tower for some unwise comments and is said to have revised Sir Walter Raleigh's *History of the World* while there. However, an enterprise of more local interest was his organization of a morris dance including twelve centenarians for the entertainment of the King. Doubtless nowadays the Society for Something or Other would prevent the employment of senior citizens in such a way, but it was surely a fine tribute to Herefordshire in the seventeenth century (and probably to the home-made cider of those days) that it could provide twelve centenarians capable of performing the morris.

Tucked away above the valley is Bacton, a rural retreat which was the birthplace of Blanche Parry, maid of honour to Queen Elizabeth I. In the church is Blanche's monument, which shows her kneeling before the Queen, and although the proportions of the two figures are disturbing, it is interesting because it is one of the few statues of the queen carved in her lifetime, and therefor might be a better likeness than most. There is a long inscription, apparently written by Blanche, which ends with the lines:

> So that my time I thus dyd passe awaye
> A maede in courte and never no mans wyffe
> Sworne of Quene Ellsbeths hedd chamber allwaye
> Wthe maeden quene a maede dyd ende my lyffe

Further up the Golden Valley are Vowchurch and Turnastone, two little places separated by a bridge over the Dore, which at this point is no more than a stream. There is a local tale that the churches were built by two sisters who quarrelled about building a church, with the result that each set about building her own, one declaring "I vow my church will be completed before you turn a stone of yours". A pleasing if improbable explanation of the names of the two places and the fact that there are two churches within sight of each other.

Turnastone is the smaller of the two villages with a shop-cum-garage which still displays one of those large enamelled Raleigh advertising signs of the 1920s which show a cyclist waving as he passes a milestone, in this case indicating 'Hereford 10 miles'. Turnastone's church is a small Norman building with a seventeenth-century bell turret; inside it has a very simple appearance, which is accentuated by the unvarnished pews. It fits the village admirably.

Vowchurch is not so tightly grouped, with houses spread over a wide area and some by the common above the valley. The church makes quite an effective picture with its prominent black-and-white turret and small spire set by a stone bridge over the Dore. It has a striking interior with a dark screen with crude carvings which might represent Adam and Eve, and an array of timbers forming a framework inside the church, which appears to have been intended to support the roof, although one of the uprights was found to be hanging from its upper joint.

Of all the Golden Valley villages, Peterchurch is the most unfortunate, for it seems to have lost its character, perhaps due to the fact that it is mainly along the B4348 whereas the other villages are tucked away off it. But it will always have a special place in my memories, for on one occasion when I visited it I asked a lad of eight or nine years what was along the path going down from the church. He looked at me carefully and then confidentially shared his secret, "There's a cat and four kittens down there." As an afterthought he added that the path also led to a farm. My map was more helpful for it showed that the path led over the Dore to Hinton, which, as 'Hinniton', had been the home of the monks brought to Peterchurch in 786 by Offa to found the church in the area.

As Offa pushed the boundary of his kingdom westwards, he

introduced Christianity and his power was so great that when he applied to the Pope for an archbishop for his own territory, the Bishop of Lichfield was raised to that position. The party of missionaries which set up their headquarters at Peterchurch therefore had a specially high standing and included an Italian bishop from Rome. Their headquarters, Peter Church, was built of stone from the first. When it was rebuilt by the Normans in 1130 the original shape and size was retained and it is a surprising survival of the design of church which was fashionable in Rome at the time it was first built. Instead of the usual chancel arch dividing the church into two sections, there are three arches dividing it into four.

The use of these is explained in an unusually interesting church guide by the Reverend John C. de la Tour Davies. This is a model for other parish guides, for it makes the church a living building rather than a mere collection of architectural terms. He explains that the apsidal east end with the altar was reserved for the officiating clergy; the next compartment, the Solea and Presbytery, was for the Prior and those monks who were clergymen; next came the Choir; and finally the Nave. The skill of the early builders is shown by the fact that a whisper made at the focal point of the apse can be heard clearly throughout the church.

On the wall over the south door there is a tablet showing a fish wearing a gold chain, which local folklore has associated with a story of a lost necklace which was found on a fish caught in the river. The vicar points out that in earlier times baptisms were carried out at St. Peter's Well and the fish could therefore represent one kept there, a custom in a number of Welsh parishes.

This ancient church has a modern spire of fibre glass and steel, which in 1972 replaced the old spire which had to be taken down in 1949 as it was unsafe. This new spire is of disappointingly ordinary design and perhaps at some time will be replaced by a more original form.

The largest of the Golden Valley villages is Dorstone, an intriguing place with a network of little roads among which, with the aid of some not very helpful signposts, it is easy to get lost.

Despite having made a number of visits I still often circle it several times before I arrive at the little green surrounded by stone buildings. On a tall post there is a sundial of unusual design; the dial is tipped so that it is parallel with the equator and with the gnomon at right angles to it, and the hour spacings round the dial are equal distances apart.

Dorstone is one of those places which repay close attention. There are some interesting dwellings converted from old buildings near the church, and opposite it some noble chimneys hidden among the trees.

The hills to the south of Dorstone climb to the 1,000 feet mark and I have been caught in a heavy snowstorm up there which made driving practically impossible, while the sun was still shining down in the valley. There are tiny half-forgotten places such as Urishay; St. Margarets, whose church has a finely carved screen; and Michaelchurch Escley, a rather attractive place to find in the hills, which has a faded wall painting of Christ surrounded by tools of various trades in the church, and Michaelchurch Court approached by an avenue a mile long.

On the hill north of Dorstone is Arthur's Stone, a chamber formed of side stones and a capstone, which is the remains of a burial mound. On the north side of this ridge is the valley of the upper Wye, here a more placid stream than in its more famous scenic stretches further down, although highly regarded by fishermen. Apparently it is not so well thought of by the inhabitants, for most of the villages are very wary of it and keep to higher ground.

Although much of Bredwardine clusters round the attractive red brick inn, the village does break the local pattern and wanders off down the road towards the river. A pleasant green lane on the right leads to the church set up on a knoll. Kilvert, the famous diarist, spent his last two years there; he was only 39 when he died in 1879. The church itself has an eleventh-century nave and a thirteenth-century chancel, with a curious kink in the south wall where they meet, which is so great that the altar is hidden from the view of a portion of the congregation. There is no explanation for this oddity, but as the chancel is the later structure I wonder if perhaps the builders were trying to orientate it more accurately, for such an awkward join is not likely to have been the result of a mistake.

Despite its quiet position, Bredwardine has its gaiety, for two local hunts hold their point-to-point meetings there; and during spells of fine weather the river bank by the great six-arched bridge becomes almost like an inland resort, with the river full of young lads and lasses; the latter would have caught Kilvert's eye. On the far side, in contrast to all this activity, is Brobury with another of Herefordshire's redundant churches lost among trees.

Along the way to Hereford the road keeps away from the river and runs under wooded slopes. The tree-studded Moccas Park is a rare sight in a county which has few large country estates. The park has an intriguing fence, with uprights of irregular height, which looks as if it had been put up by a novice, except that such consistent irregularity could only be achieved by design! It is said that the idea was to perplex the deer in the park who are supposed to be unable to judge height accurately, but as deer are used to jumping natural obstacles, which are often irregular, the principle does not seem to be sound; though the fact that they are inside the fence perhaps proves it. Part of the fence is sunk in a ditch like a ha-ha and possibly the whole boundary was originally of this type.

The village, which takes its name from the Welsh words 'Moch' and 'Rhos', meaning Pig and Moor or Swamp, is scattered, but has a nice grouping round the post office. Moccas Court has a simple exterior, but some fine rooms inside, and it stands in grounds landscaped by Capability Brown. The only other example of his work in the county is at Berrington Hall. The church standing nearby was built in the twelfth century of the local calcareous tufa. This is stone formed by the deposit of limestone from water on to vegetable matter, and is the principle by which articles left in the drip of water at the Wells at Knaresborough and Matlock are 'turned to stone'. There is a tufa house near Matlock which is hailed as a rarity and said to have been built by a man who believed that the holey nature of the stone would insulate the house. It is therefore surprising to find it used on such a large scale at Moccas. Although restored, the church is a fine example of a small Norman building and as striking in its way as Kilpeck.

Blakemere has a much more modest air about it. There is a very small and simple church with a black-and-white cottage called the 'Old Vicarage' adjoining it. Blakemere House across the way is of moderate size, but here we are back in the typical Herefordshire scale of things.

The glory of Tyberton has departed. The eighteenth-century Tyberton Court has been demolished and now only the church remains to recall the names of past owners of the Court. In an area where most churches are of stone, it was curiously built of brick in 1720, being completely new except for the original door-way. However, inside there are box pews, a two-decker pulpit and apsidal panelling behind the altar which is believed to have been designed by John Wood, famous for his work at Bath. The clue to his association with an area so far away is the monu-ments, many of which are to Brydges. A member of this family the Duke of Chandos, was the early patron of John Wood, and in the late 1720s engaged him to build the now demolished Tyberton Court. The church has an unusual lectern in the shape of an angel, whose outstretched wings make a support for the Bible; and in the churchyard there is an elegant cross which has a thin, tapering shaft and a small, gabled head with the crucifixion on one side and on the other a seated Madonna with the Child standing on her knee. According to Aymer Vallance's *Old Crosses and Lychgates*, the cross head was found in use as a finial at the end of the church and restored to the shaft in 1915.

There is a similar cross, but not in such good state of preserva-tion, at neighbouring Madley which, again according to Vallance, was found in the effects of a Mr. Robert Clarke of Hereford and returned to its church at about the same time. This village is a pleasant example of how a place can grow gracefully. Along the road there are some good black-and-white cottages, and these continue round the church, behind which there is an unexpectedly large modern development tucked away. Most visitors never realize the additions that have been made. By separating the old from the modern homes there is no clash of styles. The church is a fine, spacious place with a long arcaded nave and an apsidal chancel, beneath which there is a crypt, which is now prosaicly used as a heating chamber.

Nearer to Hereford, a road goes over Honeymoor Common towards the Wye and reaches Eaton Bishop. It is only four miles to the outskirts of the city, but at the little corner by the church there is a peace which could be expected in the heart of the countryside. Opposite the church is a fine large house, Martins Croft, which used to be the vicarage, and adjoining this is another quite considerable house. It is most unusual to see two such large houses built as a semi-detached pair in the country where there was plenty of space for building in the past. Local legend has it that a former vicar being charged with the care of his brother who was rather difficult, built this house for him so that he would be under his wing, but not a thorn in his flesh. I hope this is true.

In the church, the greatest treasure is the stained glass in the East Window, which is reputed to be the best of its time (the fourteenth century) in the county. This window has recently been cleaned and releaded and it has an almost jewel-like clarity and brilliance. The treatment has brought back the original glory of the window and it must certainly send many people away filled with an ambition to have the glass in their own church treated in the same way.

Nearer towards Hereford is Clehonger, which starts with a modern development at Gorsty Common, but has a green by the church which is so neat that it is easy to see why it had won the title of the 'Best Kept Herefordshire Village'. In the church, brasses to Sir John Barre who died in 1483, and his wife Joan, who died in 1484, have been removed from the floor and fixed to a board on the wall. They are beautifully detailed and Joan is turning towards her husband in a most lifelike pose that shows off her butterfly headdress and other attractions in a striking manner; but I have never been able to see the actual brasses, because on every occasion that I have been to Clehonger brass-rubbers have been at work.

By the time Kingstone is reached, the effect of the proximity of Hereford can at last be seen. Some good old houses and attractive cottages survive, including Bridge Court, a late Georgian brick house, but they are becoming buried by arid new buildings. What a shame that a little more care was not taken so that the additional housing did not eclipse the best of the past.

On the north side of the Wye—I must beware of writing 'bank' because most places do not keep too close company with the river—as soon as the immediate environs of Hereford are passed, there is quiet countryside. Credenhill now has a large military camp, but it has earned its place in the county annals because it was there in 1887 that H. P. Bulmer, the son of the rector, started making cider, and this originated the firm which has carried the name of Herefordshire into all parts of the country. After his first experiments he moved to Hereford, and the firm is not therefore a village industry like Westons and Symonds, but by encouraging the planting and care of orchards it has helped to maintain a traditional feature of the Herefordshire scene.

The atmosphere of Credenhill Rectory appears to encourage creative thought. A seventeenth-century rector, Thomas Traherne, wrote a number of prose works and also some poems; although these were rather a long time in reaching publication, for they were eventually 'discovered' in 1895 and not published until this century.

Kenchester's days of fame were long ago in Roman times when it was the town of Magna. There is little to see of this now although excavations show that the town covered an area of over twenty acres. Portions of mosaic floors and decorated plaster have been unearthed. It is fascinating to surmise what may lie below, for in such a rural area there is less chance of disturbance than in a town.

The post office at Mansell Lacy is one of the most photographed in the country, for it is in an old cottage with a pigeon loft built into the wall above, so that it is a positive encouragement for

L

captions about a pigeon post. In such a Rip Van Winkle of a place I was not surprised to discover one of the Fordson tractors which came over in the First World War still in running order and used for occasional jobs.

At Yazor nearby there is a complete contrast, for its sharp-looking church with a needle-like tower and spire seems completely out of keeping with the soft countryside below the wooded hillside. The church was rebuilt in 1843 to replace the older one which stands in ruins across the road. It is ironic that Foxley, the estate behind the village, was the home of Sir Uvedale Price (1747–1829) who was highly regarded for a three-volume work on the Picturesque. As well as theorizing, Sir Uvedale put his ideas into action and the results are still visible at Foxley, although the house in which he lived has now gone. Sir Walter Scott studied the work when he was planning the grounds of Abbotsford, and among other notable people who visited Foxley was Wordsworth, who stayed at Brinsop Court nearby, the home of his wife's brother, a connection which is commemorated by windows in the church there. Herefordshire was not a source of great inspiration to the poet; of the three poems he wrote at Brinsop, one was on the loss of a dove by the daughter of the rector of Bishopstone, an idyllic place with a moated grange and a small church among orchards.

Ways over the Wye along this stretch are rare, so the crossing at Bridge Sollers is useful even if it does entail several miles of lane-motoring on the south side to get to the main road. The church on its prominent site on a rise, acts as a guide to the turning; without it the little village could easily be missed. There was an earlier crossing at Byford, which is a larger place with the sixteenth-century Byford Court and a church which dates from Norman and thirteenth-century days.

The land behind rises up to Garnons Hill where at Mansell Gamage, there is the home of the Garnons and a little village with houses spaced out along the road. The church which was heavily restored, has been declared redundant and plans for its conversion to living accommodation have been prepared.

Further west, vast acres of Bulmers' orchards now stretch down to Monnington. Increasing demands for Herefordshire cider have reversed the trend to grub up orchards, and Bulmers have themselves planted over 2,000 acres of trees in the county. The big new blocks give a strange look to the countryside, because there are not the usual signs of farm activity with varied enterprises and stock in the fields. At Monnington, very strange sights may be seen, for in part of the orchards guidance wires for automatic tractors which do not need drivers have been laid and these are able to do many of the routine jobs such as spraying, and mowing the grass between the trees.

There is a rather end-of-the-world air about the road that goes down to Monnington Court and the church. For centuries there has been a tradition that Owain Glyndwr was buried under a stone in the churchyard, though it is more likely that he lies at Monnington Stradel. There is no doubt that the Tomkyns lived in the village, for they have left their mark. They rebuilt the house in 1656; and Uvedale Tomkyns and his wife Mary rebuilt the church in 1679, except for the fifteenth-century tower. Fortunately, it has been little touched since their time and it now presents an exquisite picture of the period. The simple whitewashed interior sets off the dark woodwork of the pews and screen, which has thin, twisted columns like barley sugar sticks made of treacle toffee. The coloured arms of Charles II strike a brilliant note. Only a church such as this, under the wing of a big house, could have survived so well.

Staunton on Wye is above the main road, mostly stretched along its own road with much modern development. The best thing about it is the fine view it provides. Letton has fared little better. The church has suffered too, for it was unwisely built on low ground by the river and the folly of this is shown by a mark in the porch twenty-seven inches from the ground, which records the height reached by flood water.

Whitney also suffered from floods, and the church had to be rebuilt in 1740. Now most traffic hurries past with scarcely a glance along the road to Brecon, or crosses the wooden toll bridge seeking a quiet way to Hay through Clifford which lies at the foot of the steep hillside by the river. Now a place of little consequence, there are only scant remains of the castle to hint at its earlier importance. This was one of the early castles set up by the Normans. It passed to the Cliffords by marriage and Jane Clifford, born here about 1140, became Henry II's mistress, 'the Fair Rosamond'.

The border in this area follows an erratic path, so that Hay is in Breconshire, but little Cusop at the foot of Cusop Hill is in Herefordshire. It is a real outpost, with the hills of Wales to the west, and to the east the land sloping down to the plain of Herefordshire.

10

The Black-and-White Villages

FROM the window of the room where I am writing at Staunton
on Arrow the view stretches south across the central plain of
Herefordshire to its surrounding ring of hills. Behind us is the
sheltering line of ground rising up to the Radnor and Clun Forests.
For our daily walks we choose between the lanes by the River
Arrow or climb to the top of Wapley Hill where there is one of
the hill forts reputed to have been used by Caractacus. The climate
is mild enough for there to be fields of strawberries, yet we can
see the first snows on the mountains of Wales from a viewpoint
less than a mile away. This makes it ideal for my wife and I who
never let a day go by without a walk. It does not suit everyone.
It is a place for the self-sufficient who have plenty of interests
and can cope with the difficulties arising from the lack of facilities.

The older inhabitants refer to the village as 'Stan', an echo of
its earlier names of Stanton on Arrow and Church Stanton. It
should more properly be called 'above Arrow' for the church and
the castle mound stand on top of a sharply rising knoll. Early
settlers were attracted to this position because it gave a good
view and was easily defended; later folk learned not to trust the
Arrow to keep within its banks. It is little more than a large
stream for most of the year and by the Court of Noke, an
eighteenth-century brick house with a glorious show of daffodils
in the spring, it looks shallow enough to walk across at times;
yet after only a small fall of rain here it rises rapidly and becomes
a swirling torrent, because it stretches back twenty miles or so

into the mountains of Wales and gathers the rainfall from a wide area. Flooding is rare now, but several folk in their forties in the village have told me that the houses on the south side of the river were often flooded before the River Board eased the flow to get the water away quickly.

Little is known of the history of the castle. The church was rebuilt in 1856 by the King family which then lived in Staunton Park. They must have expected the village to grow more than it has for the church is much bigger than its predecessor which is shown in a sketch hung in the church. Now the village is gently adjusting itself to the twentieth century. The changes are typical of those in many villages and are therefore worth noting for they give a picture of what is happening in the countryside. Next to the church is the school, which was closed in 1971 and sold with the school house, but was later re-opened as a private school. Opposite is a large house that used to be the village pub, but was converted into ordinary living accommodation some years ago. The post office was originally the village blacksmith's house and now looks like a child wearing her elder sister's cast-offs, because it has two bay windows which came from the big house in Staunton Park when alterations were made there, and these are so large that they reach from the ceiling almost to ground level. There are several post-war buildings, mostly bungalows, whose well-kept gardens are helping them to fit into the scene quickly. The outstanding building in the village is the handsome sixteenth-century Old Court, a grand black-and-white building with wings at either end which stands with a pleasant garden in front of it and a cluster of farm buildings old and new at its side. Fortunately those closest to the road are of mellowed stone and help to protect the character of the village. A line of poplars and some newly planted roses and shrubs in the field adjoining the buildings effectively act as a screen. So far Staunton is adapting itself very well to change, mainly because its people love it.

Stephen Graham, in one of his famous books on walking, said that an essential to the making of good coffee was the right amount of love. Going round so many villages last year I saw countless examples where a similar affection had been shown to be just as necessary in the making of a good village. Much planning is based on rules rather than on understanding and this is the reason why it so often produces arid results.

That the villagers care for their environment is evident even in minor details. Earlier this year I saw our roadman trimming the verges of the lane and I said to him, "Now Jack, don't go cutting down those campions, they make a fine show." He looked almost horror-struck at the suggestion and replied, "I've been looking after this stretch for fifteen years and I've always cut down the nettles and cow parsley and left those pink ones. That's why they've spread." No doubt some naturalist has been struggling to find a scientific explanation for the profusion of campions along the lane, but he will not have thought of such a simple solution.

In an endeavour to find at least a minor notable associated with Staunton, I consulted the invaluable records of the Wool-hope Club. These provided a rather lighthearted account of the discovery of a Roman figure in a rockery which later proved to have been built with a load of stones purchased from elsewhere. I also discovered that Wild Edric, who is said to haunt the Shropshire Hills, owned the village at the time of the Domesday survey. He was then known as Edric Sylvaticus and is said to have married a fairy whom he later lost through referring to her other-worldly connections. Some prosaic people say that Edric and his ghostly followers are no more than flocks of wild geese flying overhead at night, so it is fitting that we often hear them homing to the ponds around Staunton—or perhaps it really is Edric coming back to his old estate? The nights are usually too dark for us to be certain.

The one cloud in the sky is caused by light planes from the air-field at Shobdon nearby, a wartime base which is now used by the local aero club. It also houses a new industrial concern which converts small timber from Forestry Commission plantations into wood wool slab by cutting it into shavings and mixing it with cement. This is one of the new industries resulting from the

Commission's efforts. It may seem wasteful to grow trees to produce shavings, but the thinning has to be done if the remainder of the trees are to reach their full size. The factory also serves a useful function by providing employment for men in the area and thus helping to keep the district alive.

It is a pity that just a little money could not be found to move the ghastly remains of the huts beside the airfield which were used by Polish servicemen during the war. The tidying up of this area could be looked upon as a way of expressing gratitude for the help of these wartime allies and would bring a much greater improvement to the countryside than some more costly efforts of the conservationists.

Shobdon has previously had a problem with the disposal of its old buildings. In the eighteenth century, Viscount Bateman of Shobdon Court decided to pull down the old church and replace it with a more modern building. The church dated from the twelfth century and would have been as notable as the one at Kilpeck if it had been allowed to stand, for it had some very fine carvings. Viscount Bateman could not bring himself to discard the stones, and some of them were erected on a hill in the park. Exposure to the weather for two hundred years has worn the carvings considerably, but even now sufficient remains to indicate the extent of the loss which has occurred. The church which was erected in place of the older one is a marvellous confection of Rococo Gothick which stands out in the quiet Herefordshire scene. The work was carried out in 1752–6 under the supervision of the Viscount's brother, the Hon. Richard Bateman, and the style was no doubt influenced by his acquaintance with Horace Walpole. The interior is painted in pale blue and white which, with the Gothick stucco panels on the walls, creates a striking effect. As an example of its type it is outstanding, but it is also a warning of how short-lived a fashion can be and how unsuited a current trend may be for a building which will stand for centuries. When I look at it I always wish that I could see it on a summer day filled with a congregation in eighteenth-century clothes.

Shobdon village has little of interest apart from a fine range of buildings at its eastern end with the character of Cotswold stone.

At Byton, only a couple of miles north of Staunton on Arrow, there is a complete change from our gentle, south-facing scene. Byton lies on the edge of the flat Coombe Moor, a low-lying marshland with rough, reedy grass. All around are hills, often cultivated to their crests. Beside Byton one field at the top of a hill rising to 1,000 feet is regularly drilled with crops every year despite the fact that it slopes steeply. To the west of the village are the blue hills of Wales and its nearness to the border is shown by the postal address which is Byton, Presteigne, Radnorshire. It has the character of a place in the hills with small, sturdy, stone cottages, many of which are whitewashed. The church was rebuilt in the nineteenth century, using the old stones, and a Norman carving of a lamb and cross was set in the outside wall, where it will be weathered away. The approach to the church is by a rough path across a field, which cannot have been very popular with ladies in the long dresses of yesteryear. I notice that nowadays when Byton girls get married they usually prefer to come to our church at Staunton; both churches are served by the same vicar now.

This north-western tip of the county is a hilly mass merging into the mountains of Wales. There are grand views along the way to Lingen where roads come in from Cross of Tree in the east and Brierley Hill in the west, both desolate, moorland places that have the air of being in the midst of the mountains, yet it is less than five miles to the strawberry fields of Staunton. Stone and half-timbered cottages make Lingen a delightful picture in the haven of the valley. When I was there not long ago three men were dismantling a grand old five-bay, timber-built barn which was to be re-erected in Yarpole for use as a house. Stripped of roof and plasterwork, the timbers looked as clean and untouched as if they were new. The key marks which had been put on the joints when the barn was erected 400 years ago were clear enough to be used as a guide for the work. The only difficulty encountered was caused by the swelling of some of the wooden pegs used to fasten the joints, and to avoid damage in removing them, those sections were taken down complete. The fact that the material could be so readily re-used was a great tribute to the early builders.

The church overlooks farms and is very much a part of the village. A certificate that the work of beautifying the church was consecrated by Bishop Sara on 28th July 1957 lists a large team of parishioners. Perhaps this is because it has the true atmosphere of a country church; for although it was rebuilt last century the original simplicity was not lost and the sixteenth-century benches with the marks of their makers' tools were retained.

This area seems remote now, but for centuries the main road from London to Aberystwyth and Central Wales ran along the present B4362 road to Presteigne, which explains how Byron came to stay at Kinsham Court, and why Wordsworth and Shelley were at Eywood in the hills above Titley.

In such country there is a wide variety of scene and character in the villages. Lyonshall is worth a visit for the view from the church, which is perched high above the A44 road overlooking parkland. From the porch, the village lies directly below and then the scene stretches across to the hills behind Bredwardine in the upper Wye Valley, giving a grand top-of-the-world feeling. Behind the church are the remains of the castle surrounded by its still water-filled moat; unfortunately it is so overgrown that little can now be seen.

At Almeley, in contrast, the motte and bailey of the old castle by the church has been carefully cleared of trees so that it is possible to see the shape perfectly. This arrangement of church and primitive castle together on a hilltop is frequently found in this area and was a necessary precaution in the days when attacks were to be feared. The church itself has been rather over-restored, but the attractive roof over the rood painted in panels with Tudor roses survives from the early sixteenth century.

Nearby at Woonton is a cottage almost dwarfed by its yew hedge which is topped by a topiary aeroplane and a squirrel. Mr. Mifflin told me that in 1936 he cut back the two yews of which it is formed so that they grew together to form a twenty-foot high wind-break for his garden, which is above the road level. The two trunks were allowed to grow on, and in 1946 he decided to form one into a squirrel and the other into an areoplane in view of the fact that his son was in the R.A.F. At such a height the trees were slow to develop and this final stage took many years, but eventually his patience was rewarded. Now he wishes it was nearer to the ground.

That energetic recorder of English buildings, Nikolaus Pevsner, comments with relief of Eardisley that "the village has a proper street, which is not all that frequent in Herefordshire", and I have a feeling that the straggling form of many of the villages in these two counties must have been a trial to one of such precise disposition. The only pity is that the street of Eardisley is the A4111 which is quite busy as Herefordshire roads go, for the village deserves to be left in peace. There is a specially delightful corner by the 'Tram Inn', which takes its name from the old tram railway long since closed. The farm opposite has a grand long timber-framed barn, the possibilities of which are demonstrated at the far end of the village beside the church where a similar type of barn was converted into four houses in 1965. I had a look round one of these homes and was very impressed by the skilful manner in which a building that had been in use as a barn for centuries has been converted into pleasing and modern accommodation. The old beams inside were in magnificent condition and the present homes would surprise the generations of farm workers who had carried produce into the barn. This is a really worthwhile conversion, because the barn would not fit in with modern farming methods, yet if it had been dismantled it would have been a great loss to the village. Now it is saved; the farmer and builder have no doubt made a profit; and the four occupiers are very proud of homes that are 'different', yet do not have the disadvantages which that term often conceals.

The church has a font as remarkable as the famous one at Castle Frome, with carvings showing two figures fighting, the Harrowing of Hell and a large lion. These are in the style of those at Kilpeck and the whole design is most exciting. Perhaps it is not what one would choose for the decoration of a font to be used for christening young babies, but in earlier days this ceremony took place at a later age than nowadays. The carvings give the impression that the unknown artist was delighted to have the large area of the bowl-shaped font to decorate, and really let himself go. He must have been proud of the result and for 800 years it has delighted people, which is a very satisfying achievement.

Once a year the people of Eardisley let their hair down and stetson-hatted cowboys canter along the street on the occasion of the annual 'Stampede' which includes riding the bucking bullock and other events which are usually associated with the Wild West rather than with a quiet Midland county.

Willersley and Winforton along the Brecon road are typical 'farm' villages, quiet places with the stamp of the yeoman rather than the squire or the noble earl. The church at Willersley is one of those in the county which were declared redundant and offered for sale for conversion. I picked up an old man in the road nearby and gave him a lift into Kington. On the way we talked of the church and he told me that although he had not attended the services all that often, to him the church was a special place, for he had married and buried his wife there and he did not feel that it was right for people to live in it. Perhaps in time the village's attachment to its church will fade and conversion to other uses will be more acceptable, but whether it is worth the church incurring this loss in its standing for a mere palmful of silver is a question that only time will answer. Certainly it is a sad loss for the villages concerned.

Along the A4112 towards Leominster there now comes a string of delightful places. Kinnersley stands on a slope with a grand view across the valley to the hills on the other side of the Wye; like many of the other views mentioned in this chapter this faces south and is often hazy, but on a day after showers, especially with a north-westerly wind, the scene becomes crystal clear and distance seems to shrink so that features far away can be picked out with ease. Kinnersley Castle is an Elizabethan house which

was probably a remodelling of an earlier castle. Although it is a
large building with a five-storeyed tower it is almost hidden behind trees and the church. The church is also quite large and has
a dominating tower which rises like a cliff to a saddleback roof.
The interior is rich with decorations painted on the walls of the
nave and on the roof of the chancel, and some handsome memorials, including a fine alabaster monument to Francis Smallman of
Stuart days, and a classical monument to Lady Morgan (died
1764) showing her bust on a medallion which is supported by an
angel. This church comes as a striking contrast to others of the
district, which are very simple, and speaks of generations of
wealthy squires living in the great house nearby.

They are all forgotten figures now, while every visitor to the
county knows of John Abel, the King's Carpenter who is buried
in the churchyard of the simple little church at Sarnesfield. He
designed his own tomb which is beside the porch. The inscription
can just be made out in a good light and begins:

> This craggy stone a covering is for an Architects bed
> That lofty buildings raised high, yet now lays low his head.

He obviously had no mean opinion of his ability when he died
at the age of ninety-seven in 1674, and he would be even more
delighted with his reputation now, for many buildings are credited
to him which he probably did not build. Any structure of merit
is claimed to be his to add a little of his fame to it. Oddly enough
he did not win his title of 'The King's Carpenter' in recognition of
his buildings, but because at the time of the siege of Hereford in
1645 during the Civil War he built a mill for the city. The outstanding example of his work to be seen now is Grange Court used
as a Civic Office in Leominster. Originally this stood in the main
street of the town, the upper storey being used as a session
chamber and the ground floor being an open market hall. When a
new town hall was built in 1855 this building was sold and the
timbers lay in a builder's yard till they were purchased by Mr.
Arkwright who re-erected them in the Grange, built in the ground
floor and converted it for domestic use. In 1939, to prevent its

sale to America, the council bought the building back and it is now one of the most attractive council premises in the country. Abel's other great work is the restoration of Dore Abbey, where his screen is a great feature. It is known that he also designed the market halls at Brecon and Kington, but both of these have been demolished. Despite John Abel's great reputation, very little is known about him and few of his works can be identified. The church where he lies is a delightfully simple place which gains some peace from the fact that it is by the A4112 at a point where there are double white lines and only a small area in which to park. Would John Abel have been pleased with this detachment or would a man who wrote his own epitaph have preferred his burial place to be more accessible?

Weobley lies in a wide, flat valley and having no rising ground on which to set the church, the builders gave it a tall tower and a great spire so that it could be seen from afar. It is also a dominating feature in the village itself, making a striking focal point at the end of the main street. Weobley is one of the best black-and-white villages in the county—indeed one of the best in the country— with many timber-built houses and a number where the black 'beams' have been painted on to whitewashed brick walls. This shocks some people, but if it improves the look of the village it does not seem to be a matter for protest; many girls look all the better for a little added paintwork and only the grimmest puritan complains about that.

Weobley always has an air of peace as if it is posing for the many pictures which are taken of its main street, which is one of the few that I know which make a good photograph from either direction: from the top of the village the street tapers inwards to the 'Red Lion Inn', behind which the spire of the church soars upwards; while from the bottom of the village looking the other way there is a fine grouping of timber-built houses. A walled garden in the middle of the street by the 'Salutation Inn' marks the site of an island of buildings which were burnt down some years ago. Although the loss of what were some grand old buildings is regrettable, it has given the street a fine air. Until 1832,

Weobley was a pocket borough with two M.P.s. The most famous of these, Colonel Birch, is found in the church, where his statue stands in a striking pose. When the Civil War began, John Birch was a Bristol merchant, but he quickly made progress in Cromwell's army, capturing Hereford and being made Governor of that town. Later he had a rather chequered career, for he was not willing to follow the party line blindly and he quarrelled with Cromwell, being several times imprisoned, and eventually helped in the restoration of the Stuarts. Among his projects was a scheme for the rebuilding of London after the Great Fire, but this was not adopted.

I had an interesting correspondence with Prebendary A. L. Moir about the niches in the base of the cross at Weobley. He said that he believed that three of these were merely decorative, but that the fourth was probably used in the Palm Sunday celebrations when the pyx containing the Host would be brought from the church in procession and placed in it. There are thirty-nine crosses with similar niches in Herefordshire. He also passed on a less reputable tale that if one went to Weobley churchyard at midnight and walked slowly round the cross seven times repeating the Lord's Prayer backwards the devil would immediately appear. Nowadays I expect he would be in the guise of the local policeman asking what you thought you were a-doing-of!

It may appear strange that in the stretch of countryside between Weobley and the A4110 there should be a number of interesting villages, while the A49, which is the modern main road, should be a barren stretch. The secret is that originally the A4110 was the more important road and locally it is still referred to as 'the old Hereford road'. This explains the previous importance of Wormsley, south-east of Weobley, which now seems a remote place for the large house, The Grange, where Richard Payne Knight and Thomas Knight were born. Their grandfather was a Shropshire ironmaster whose fortune enabled the two brothers to gain fame in different spheres. Richard was an antiquarian who spent several years in Italy where he studied and gathered a collection of antiques. On his return to the county he settled down, built

Downton Castle and was later M.P. for Hereford for twenty years. Thomas became a horticulturist and produced new strains of apples, pears, plums and other fruit, including the famous Elton cherries. Although the brothers spent much of their lives elsewhere, they are both buried in the church.

There are big houses at King's Pyon too, a delightful place that wanders down a hill from the church to a little stream and then up the other side. One of the best houses is the white-painted Brook House set above its farmyard, in which there is a pond and a black-and-white dovecot making a charming picture. Neighbouring Canon Pyon has divided its loyalties. The older houses stand by the church near Pyon Hill in a rural group, while down a lane on the A4110 the modern houses enjoy easier communications, but are disturbed by the traffic.

Burghill, nearer to Hereford, successfully hides down a lane. A large church in a raised churchyard looks as if it is standing back from the normal business of the village. Beside the path there are twelve old yews which are known as the twelve apostles; some of them have now died after being trimmed rather too harshly, and beside each a young 'apostle' is being grown, standing like page boys at present. The unofficial sexton, busy with a rotary mower rather than the traditional scythe, told me that he would like to see them all done away with for they were relics of the days "when you had to be gloomy to go to Heaven". He would have preferred to have seen something more cheerful and we discussed the selection of flowering trees which would give a summer-long sequence. The church has a brass to Robert Masters who died in 1619 and who travelled with Thomas Cavendish "To Virginia and afterwards about ye globe of ye whole worlde", a journey which is commemorated by an engraving of the globe. He would still like this pleasant little village if he returned and he would not find too many changes.

A little over two miles east of Weobley is Dilwyn, another of the villages built on the familiar S-shaped squiggle plan. This may have been pleasant in the days of horse-drawn traffic, but for years poor Dilwyn suffered grievous bodily harm on a number of occasions when lorries got out of control at night as they tried to follow the road squirming between the houses, with the result that one or other of the buildings was damaged. During the time I have been writing this book a bypass has been built to take traffic round Dilwyn. The effect is to miraculously bring it a peace it has not known for many years. Midway between the village and Pembridge is Luntley Court, one of the best of the black-and-white buildings standing in a little oasis in the lanes, with a dovecot and a group of cottages, to make one of those set pieces which is so delightful because nothing intrudes to break the illusion that one is back in the seventeenth century.

From Luntley Court the lane winds on in the way that only Herefordshire lanes can wind till it comes out to the A44 at Pembridge. The centre of the village is the triangular market 'square' behind the 'New Inn', which was new in the seventeenth century. There is a little market hall, which is simply constructed with a tiled roof on eight sturdy oak pillars. It is said that the loft of the building was used as a lock-up, but it does not look as if it would have held anyone for very long. It must have had a sobering effect on customers at the 'New Inn', or perhaps they moved along to the 'Greyhound Inn' on the main road? This has close-set upright timbers which gives it a different mood to most of the county's black-and-white buildings; it really deserves more notice than it receives, but there is so much to see in the village that most people only have time to take in a general view. There is the elevated shop known as 'Ye Olde Steppes'; the old forge with its archway now blocked up; houses with cruck beams; two old almshouses; and at the west end of the village there is even a timber-framed house with uncharacteristic red brick infilling. The pavements rise as much as nearly two feet six inches above the road in places. Yet time and understanding have blended all this disorder into a pleasant unity. Pembridge should be required viewing for all planners who refuse to allow changes from the existing shapes and sizes.

Above all these attractions is the churchyard with the church and its bell tower, one of the seven detached towers in the county and certainly the most striking. It has a broad, low stone base above which is a wooden tower rising in stages to a little spire; the whole erection being reminiscent of a pagoda. Inside, a sturdy frame of timber to support the clock and the bells is equally impressive.

The Pembridge bellringers are a friendly team. I was watching them ringing one Sunday when a visitor asked if he could take part. He was a novice and instead of taking advantage of his lack of experience as some teams tend to do, they coached him so that he was able to feel at home and gained confidence. This spirit seems to fill the church, for a few years ago a music and flower festival was staged and this was a great financial success because it was supported by the efforts of all the folk in the village, and no expenses were incurred by getting outsiders to do things.

There have been quite a number of new houses built in Pembridge, but they have been so discreetly placed in groups away from the existing streets that they do not affect the general appearance of the village. A little thought in making similar plans in other places could have equally happy results.

Eardisland, a few miles nearer to Leominster, is the only one of the villages along this stretch of the Arrow to be built near to the river. Searching for a reason I discovered a map of the county prepared during a survey that was carried out just after the war; this showed that this was the only section of the valley in the area not subject to flooding. By the bridge in the village, there is a stretch with lawns coming to the water's edge, which tempts many visitors to take pictures; as an added inducement there is a pair of swans which seem to know when their presence is required by photographers. The rest of the village is not quite so outstanding because it has been diluted with new buildings, but this is only because the general standard of the county is so high. In other parts of the country a village with half the number of old houses would become a five-star attraction. There is the 'Swan Inn', for instance, with its porch using old wheels for sidelights, which is as attractive inside with its collection of horse brasses and, over the window where they are often missed, some old spirit jars which were used for transporting neat spirit to be diluted in the inn.

The final section of this chapter goes into the country north of Eardisland which gradually changes from the soft central plain of Herefordshire to the hillier border area. Kingsland, set along the B4360, is a mixture of old and new, the many old black-and-white buildings making it easy to picture the village in earlier days. The church stands back from the village and is approached by a small lane which stops suddenly at the churchyard to reveal a surprisingly large and high building. A lady who was putting up the numbers of the hymns for the next service claimed that it was high enough for a cathedral, and I had to agree. She also told me that the electric lights had been put up right in that lofty roof and could only be reached by going along a catwalk among the trusses, a feat so perilous that it was difficult to get anyone to do it. Leading off the north porch is the mysterious little Volka Chapel, a small cell which is now furnished as a sanctuary, but whose original purpose is not known.

Kingsland is remembered as the site of the Battle of Mortimer's Cross and at the north end of the village is a monument, which was erected by public subscription in 1799, telling how Edward Mortimer defeated Henry VI in an "obstinate and bloody battle on 2nd February 1461". Edward's forces of some 23,000 camped in the Great West Field at Kingsland and awaited the Lancastrians coming down from Shobdon and Aymestrey. The battle was one of those won by quick action and even quicker thinking: a successful charge by a Lancastrian force led by the Earl of Pembroke that went on too far; and a speedy reply by the Yorkists that defeated the other body of their foes, so that by the time Pembroke's men came back it was too late. On that short February day, over 4,000 men died. It all seems pointless now in this peaceful corner and one can only say with old Kaspar, "t'was a famous victory."

To the east of Mortimer's Cross is Lucton gathered round its church in what used to be a charming picture, but now the church has been declared redundant. Much the grandest building hereabouts is Lucton School on the hill above the village. This was founded in 1708 by John Pierrepont whose statue in wood, painted white, stands in a niche over the porch; above him there is a single-handed clock, bearing the date 1708, which still has its original works and keeps good time. Although a modest looking place the school has a wide reputation. A gardener who was mowing the lawns said that he had known it all his life and that even while he was a lad pupils from Africa had attended it, showing how far its fame had spread.

Nearby are the grounds of Croft Castle where the Crofts lived from the time of the Domesday Book until about 1750 when it was sold to a member of the Knight family of ironmasters; in 1923 the family bought the estate back and resumed their long occupation, selling it to the National Trust in 1957. Most of the exterior dates from the fourteenth and fifteenth centuries, but it was modified over the years, particularly in the mid-eighteenth century by the family of Thomas Johnes of Hafod.

A new housing estate has recently been built at Yarpole, but this is discreetly away from the older part so that although this will no doubt be 'smartened up' it will still be possible to savour the original delight of the village as I remember it over the years. A little stream joins a typically Herefordshire tangle of roads and cottages to make a picture which is especially dreamlike in spring when the gardens are full of flowers. Space is at a premium with everything crowded together; even the detached belfry of the church, which is similar to though smaller than the one at Pembridge, is squeezed into the churchyard in front of the church.

Eye, as its name suggests, is on an island of land formed by two streams, and although it is only a tiny village it is one of the places which I always recommend visitors to see. Eye Manor, built in 1680 for Ferdinando Gorges, a Barbados slave trader, is modest enough from the outside, but the interior fully lives up to the exotic name of the builder, with ceilings which have some of the richest decoration in the country. In large panels are flowers, fruit and figures modelled by hand in plaster and in some cases almost detached from the ceiling. This alone would make a visit worth while, but the present owners, Mr. and Mrs. Sandford, are a delightful couple who have brought their own skills to add to the attractions of the house. Christopher Sandford ran the Golden Cockerel Press before the war, a private press that produced exquisite limited editions of books, and there is a display of these in one room; his wife was one of those responsible for the revival of interest in corn dollies, and she has arranged a display which shows not only the traditional styles of various areas but also some special creations she has evolved using the old methods. My own favourites are the figures and animals she has produced in cut straw in the Scandinavian style. These have a fascinating simplicity.

A mile away is Berrington Hall, standing in a great park that runs alongside the A49. This is such a perfect landscape that it obviously had to be man-made, and it was in fact laid out by Lancelot Capability Brown, the maestro of this type of work. The house was built by his son-in-law, Henry Holland, in 1778–81, and is a grand affair of pink sandstone with a simple exterior. Inside there is an air of quiet grandeur in the great rooms, some of which have painted ceilings. The house is perhaps rather out of keeping with the simple Herefordshire scene, but it was built for Thomas Harley, who had been Lord Mayor of London and probably acquired rather grand tastes while there. In London he came into conflict with John Wilkes, whose supporters broke the windows of his carriage and of the Mansion House. Thomas Harley is buried in the little church at Eye next to Eye Manor. This is dark with many arches and small windows. The many memorials to past owners of Berrington Hall and its predecessor, mostly rather grand with recumbent figures, attendant mourners and angels, give it a sombre atmosphere; it is the sort of church in which it is terribly difficult to imagine a wedding.

Poor Orleton was being developed when I last visited it. Perhaps in time it will settle down again. Meanwhile the old black-and-white houses stand aside, rather worried about it all. Even more worried would be Harry Thomas Proctor, born in Cincinnatti Ohio in 1847, in whose honour the church was restored in

1956 by a gift from Rodney Proctor. There are memorial stones to a number of Proctors of the eighteenth century and the old man must often have dreamt of the village of which he had been told so much.

Finally at the extreme edge of the county in this direction is Richards Castle, which is partly over the border into Shropshire. The modern village is by the road and makes a pleasant, if not noteworthy feature. Its church was built in 1891–2 and makes a striking picture against the hillside. The old village climbs uphill to the scant remains of the castle and the well-preserved old church. The castle was built by the Norman, Richard FitzScrob, who came to the country before William the Conqueror and was granted the manor by Edward the Confessor in an attempt to contain the Welsh. The church is a low, squat building, crouching as if to avoid the wind, with a square detached belfry beside it. It is now used for burials, and there are such wide views from the churchyard that one has the feeling that it must be half-way to Heaven, but this is due to the land suddenly falling away, for the map shows that it is not above the 600 feet mark.

The last section of the county lies north of Mortimer's Cross along the A4110. Aymestrey is little more than an incident along the road with a pleasant corner by the bridge over the Lugg where a lane leads over the hills to Lingen. At Wigmore the road is the main street and rises up to the junction with the Ludlow road on the east and a lane to the church on the west. It is one of those places which create a pleasant general impression, but where the details disappoint. But the church is on an exciting, cliff-like site above the village. Herringbone masonry in the north wall of the nave shows its early origin. There is a dramatic view to the north where the land drops down surprisingly to give the site a brooding watchfulness. Behind it are the ruins of Wigmore Castle which was owned by the Mortimers when they were one of the great families of the land, but its origins go back much further, for it was one of the castles founded by King Alfred's daughter. Down below at Adforton there are remains of Wigmore Abbey, founded by the Mortimers. Great days there were at Wigmore, the most glorious when Edward of York set out for the great battle at Mortimer's Cross which ended in victory and the Crown. I've driven through Wigmore many times and it has always been just a pleasant village, then one day when a north-westerly gale was blowing I went up to the churchyard and, clinging to the neck strap of my camera for support, I looked out across the scene to the north. Comfortable little present-day Wigmore melted away and for a few minutes I was back in the early grand days of the Mortimers. This is one of those timeless places that never lose their magic.

In the hills behind Wigmore is part of the great new Mortimer Forest replacing the older woodland with quick-growing conifers. Ludlow Castle used to take 600 cords of firewood and 4,000 faggots from Wigmore Rolls every year. Some idea of the way in which the old woodlands of England were used up can be obtained from the fact that in 1791 Edward Harris estimated that in the previous thirty years over £200,000 worth of oak had been sold to the Navy from Shropshire, and he then doubted that there was enough remaining to make a seventy-gun ship. Scares about dwindling resources are not solely a twentieth-century phenomenon. Further inroads on the timber were made at Bringewood where iron-ore from Titterstone Clee was smelted in the eighteenth century, when Richard Knight of Madeley in Shropshire saw the opportunity and moved to the district to make his fortune.

His grandson, Richard Payne Knight, the antiquarian born at Wormsley Grange (mentioned earlier in this chapter), built Downton Castle between 1772 and 1780 on a dramatic site overlooking the River Teme. This is a strange intrusion in an area so rich in English history, for it was based on the semi-fortified houses seen in French paintings of the time. The interior is magnificently classical with porphyry columns and a carpet made in Vienna.

Where the Clun meets the Teme is Leintwardine near the old Roman site of Bravinium. But there is nothing of the historic atmosphere in present-day Leintwardine, where a happy street which always seems colourful goes down to a grand old stone bridge, where the river foams dramatically after rain.

And so to Brampton Bryan. It was by sheer chance in planning this book that Brampton Bryan became the last village to be mentioned, but as I stood in the centre of it in the mellow light of a summer evening, I realized that here was the perfect summary of the two counties. Blended by the harmony of time, there is nearly every type of cottage to be found in the area. Thatch, stone, brick, timber-framed—almost an encyclopaedia of building styles—yet all sitting comfortably by each other round the green. On the north side of the village is Brampton Bryan Hall and, behind it, the ruins of the castle begun in the thirteenth century by Bryan de Brampton whose name was taken by the village. In the fourteenth century the estate passed to the Harleys by marriage and they rebuilt the castle. Its days of glory came in the Civil War when Sir Robert Harley was away fighting with the Commonwealth Army and it was defended by his wife, Lady Brilliana, whose reply to calls to surrender were the brave words, "My lord bids me hold out." Later the castle was taken and the church also destroyed, which explains why it is rather disappointing compared with many in the counties, because it was rebuilt in a rather severe Puritan style.

The grandson of this couple, Robert Harley, Earl of Oxford, was Chief Secretary of State from 1704 to 1708 and held other high offices. A recently published book summed up his political career by saying that at a time when politics was often corrupt he showed an honesty and steadfastness which came from his deep faith and his country background. Even in the midst of affairs of state he had a thought for other things and gathered together that famous collection, the Harleian Manuscripts, which is now in the British Museum.

Two counties with their roots in history and a true appreciation of the basic values of life. They have preserved their virtues through many troubles. Perhaps the last word should be with a local police superintendent who looked out over the scene from my house and said, "When this part of England is lost to 'progress' the only thing to do will be to emigrate."

Index